STEALTH

ATTACK

PROTECTING YOURSELF AGAINST
SATAN'S PLAN TO DESTROY YOUR LIFE

RAY PRITCHARD

MOODY PUBLISHERS
CHICAGO

All Scripture quotations, unless otherwise indicated, are taken from the *Holy Bible, New International Version®*. NIV®. Copyright © 1973, 1978, 1984 by International Bible Society. Used by permission of Zondervan. All rights reserved.

Scripture quotations marked NLT are taken from the *Holy Bible, New Living Translation*, copyright © 1996, 2004. Used by permission of Tyndale House Publishers, Inc., Wheaton, Illinois 60189, U.S.A. All rights reserved.

Scripture quotations marked KJV are taken from the King James Version.

Scripture quotations marked NKJV are taken from the *New King James Version*. Copyright © 1982, Thomas Nelson, Inc., Publishers. All rights reserved.

Scripture quotations marked ESV are taken from *The Holy Bible, English Standard Version*. Copyright © 2000, 2001 by Crossway Bibles, a division of Good News Publishers. Used by permission. All rights reserved.

Scripture quotations marked THE MESSAGE are from *The Message*, copyright © by Eugene H. Peterson 1993, 1994, 1995. Used by permission of NavPress Publishing Group.

Scripture quotations marked CEV are taken from the *Contemporary English Version*. Copyright © 1991, 1992, 1995 by American Bible Society. Used by permission.

Scripture quotations marked NASB are taken from the *New American Standard Bible®*, Copyright © 1960, 1962, 1963, 1968, 1971, 1972, 1973, 1975, 1977, 1995 by The Lockman Foundation. Used by permission. (www.Lockman.org)

Cover Design: Kirk DuPonce
Cover Images: Soldier–Superstock; Water–istock
Interior Design: Ragont Design
Editor: Cheryl Dunlop

Library of Congress Cataloging-in-Publication Data

Pritchard, Ray, 1952-
    Stealth attack : arming yourself against Satan's plan to destroy your life / Ray Pritchard.
        p. cm.
    Includes bibliographical references.
    ISBN-13: 978-0-8024-0989-8
    ISBN-10: 0-8024-0989-X
    1. Spiritual warfare. I. Title.

BV4509.5.P77 2007
235'.4—dc22
                                                                        2006102713

We hope you enjoy this book from Moody Publishers. Our goal is to provide high-quality, thought-provoking books and products that connect truth to your real needs and challenges. For more information on other books and products written and produced from a biblical perspective, go to www.moodypublishers.com or write to:

Moody Publishers
820 N. LaSalle Boulevard
Chicago, IL 60610

1 3 5 7 9 10 8 6 4 2

Printed in the United States of America

STEALTH

ATTACK

*This book is gratefully dedicated
to the founding board members
of Keep Believing Ministries:*

*Brian Bill
Peter Faulkner
Dave Hoy
Alan Pritchard
Cliff Raad
MaryAnn Spiegel*

CONTENTS

ACKNOWLEDGMENTS

GREG THORNTON HAD THE INITIAL VISION for this book. He also waited very patiently while I finished the manuscript. Cheryl Dunlop did a magnificent job of editing the manuscript. John and Karen Grassmick showed me much hospitality every time I came to Dallas for a visit. It has been my joy every Sunday to pray for Grant Brown, Brian Bill, Phil Newton, Davis Duggins, and Andy McQuitty as they preach the Word. B. J. Lundy, Paula DeCanter, Linda Hale, Burt and Danna Duncan deserve special thanks, along with my brother Alan for his kindness to us. Josh, Mark, and Nick have been a special source of strength, encouragement, and, above all, hope. And we thank God for bringing Josh and Leah together. In the last year Marlene and I have discovered that we have many friends—more than we can count—who love us unreasonably. It is wonderful to be loved and to know it. This is one of God's greatest gifts.

"Stay alert! Watch out for your great enemy, the devil. He prowls around like a roaring lion, looking for someone to devour."

—1 PETER 5:8 NLT

"The price of freedom is eternal vigilance."

—THOMAS JEFFERSON

INTRODUCTION

"The Christian life is not a playground; it is a battleground."

—WARREN WIERSBE

AROUND 8:30 A.M. THE PHONE RANG.
My wife was calling. "Turn on the TV. A plane has hit the World Trade Center." I don't remember much else about that day. Eventually I made my way to the church and met with the staff. That night hundreds of people gathered in the sanctuary to sing, to weep, to pray.

The world changed forever on September 11, 2001, and for those of us who lived through it, it was only the beginning. I don't remember all that I said to the congregation that night, except that I told them that terrorism had come close to us and it would come closer still in the future. In the confusion of those early hours, we had not yet heard about the heroes of United Flight 93, nor of a terror organization called al-Qaeda. The name Osama bin Laden had not yet become familiar around the world.

We had yet to live through the anthrax scare or the attack on the Taliban in Afghanistan, and the color-coded alert system was still in the future. Several years would pass before the invasion of Iraq and all the controversy that would flow from it. Still in the future were suicide bombers and shoe bombers and subway bombers and train bombers.

On that frightening day, anything seemed possible. The authorities evacuated the Sears Tower in Chicago, fearing it might be a target of a hijacked airplane. For a few days, commercial aviation came to a standstill. Tens of thousands of military personnel were called to active duty. Later scares included the power grid, the Internet, the water supply, the interstate trucking system, the food chain, every large building, football stadiums, and shopping malls. Even churches might become a target.

A target for whom? To this day the answer remains murky and multiple. A good guess would include small terror cells linked by cell phones and computers, and terrorist groups like Hezbollah, Hamas, Islamic Jihad, and, of course, al-Qaeda. They spread like zoophytes, reproducing themselves, then detaching themselves, acting sometimes alone, sometimes in concert with others.

"We are at war." That's what the president said after 9/11. He was right, and he was right again when he said that the war against terror would last for years, and it might not end in our lifetime. As I write these words, despite significant progress on many fronts, there is no end in sight.

I think I started writing this book in my mind sometime during that long day, when we all sat glued to the TV, watching with horror as billows of black smoke streamed heavenward from Lower Manhattan where the World Trade Center had once stood.

A few weeks later I stood with some friends at Ground Zero and looked at the devastation. The night before, we had prayed in front of the White House and visited the gaping wound in the side of the Pentagon. Sometime along in there, during those long days when the world seemed to turn upside down, I started thinking again about what I believe. I came to the conviction that in a world like this, where planes fly into buildings and where madmen love death more than life and blow themselves up on a crowded bus to make some sort of political point, in a world fueled by rage that defies understanding, it is time for everyone to decide what matters most, and then go and do it.

I thought about writing a book about that topic. This is not that book, but it is a step in that direction. It's a new look at an old war, a struggle that has been going on between good and evil since the beginning of time. It's about spiritual warfare in an age of terror. Since I happen to believe there is a close link between the physical and the spiritual, that what happens in the unseen realm directly affects the world around us, I have looked at the shattering events of the early years of the twenty-first century to help us understand our place in the great cosmic battle between God and the devil, light and darkness, good and evil. In that battle we are all frontline soldiers, and no one gets a vacation.

This is not a book about politics, but it does contain many references to current events. Perhaps fifty years from now—if the world as we know it still exists—what I have written may seem rather dated. If so, my answer is the one Paul gave in 1 Corinthians 10:11, that the stories of the Bible were "written down *for our instruction, on whom the end of the ages has come*" (ESV, italics added). That last phrase joins the first century with the twenty-first.

The lessons of history are lost to us unless we learn from the past and apply it to the present. Now more than ever, the end of the ages has come upon us. We must not ignore the flow of history and culture. Paul added another thought in Romans 13:11, "You know what sort of times we live in, and so you should live properly. It is time to wake up. You know that the day when we will be saved is nearer now than when we first put our faith in the Lord" (CEV). We live in apocalyptic times, when the nations are being shaken and no one can feel safe anymore. This book is my small contribution to a conviction that arose from the ashes of 9/11.

It's time to wake up.

A NEW NAME FOR A VERY OLD WAR

"Once we have a war there is only one thing to do. It must be won. For defeat brings worse things than any that can ever happen in war."

—ERNEST HEMINGWAY

ARE YOU FAMILIAR WITH THE TERM *asymmetric warfare*? The concept has received lots of news coverage in recent years as a result of the war on terrorism. The word *asymmetric* refers to something that is out of balance. In warfare it describes a situation where the combatants are not equal. Asymmetric warfare involves "the use of unconventional tactics to counter the overwhelming conventional military superiority of an adversary."[1] When two forces are severely mismatched, the weaker force must use unusual methods of warfare in order to have any hope of prevailing in the conflict.

Wars have often involved a vastly superior force against a much weaker one, but most people tend to think of warfare in terms of forces that are roughly equal. Most American wars have been examples of symmetric warfare. In World War II you had the Allied armies on one side and the German, Italian, and Japanese armies on the other side. They fought traditional battles for territory across the islands of the Pacific and across North Africa and Europe.

In the twenty-first century, a new sort of warfare has come to the forefront. Conventional armies face loosely organized terrorist cells. Here are three clear examples of asymmetric warfare. On October 3, 2000, the USS *Cole*, an American battleship equipped with the latest and most sophisticated technology, went to the harbor of Aden, Yemen, for what was meant to be a routine fuel stop. At 11:18 a.m. two men in a rubber boat approached the ship. They blew a forty-by-forty-foot hole in the side of the ship, killing seventeen American sailors and injuring thirty-nine others. The irony was that this battleship, designed to protect a carrier battle group against all threats, was powerless to stop two men in a rubber boat.

Let's suppose that you are Osama bin Laden, and you wish to strike a blow against what you regard as the visible symbol of corrupt Western capitalism. Let us further suppose that you have a handful of men at your disposal. How will you attack the World Trade Center? You could launch some sort of frontal assault, but a few armed men would never make it very far. It just can't be done. So what do you do? You train the men to commandeer commercial aircraft and fly them into the Twin Towers. And you even plan it so that the attacks are staggered, with the shock of the first tower being hit guaranteeing that the whole world will be watching when the second tower is struck.

When two planes hit the World Trade Center, a third hit the Pentagon, and another crashed into the ground in Pennsylvania, the result was more than Osama bin Laden could have dreamed. Almost three thousand people died that day.

When my wife and I had a three-hour layover in Atlanta, we decided to eat lunch at the airport. Two soldiers wearing Army fatigues sat down at the table next to us. My wife discovered they had been in Iraq and were returning for another tour of duty, so she asked how it was really going over there. "We're kicking them all over the place," one soldier said, "but you'll never hear that on the news." He said that 90 percent of the Iraqis are glad the Americans are there, 5 percent don't care, and the other 5 percent want to kill us. There is no way to stop the 5 percent because they have infiltrated every layer of Iraqi society, including the Iraqi Army we're trying to train. We have overwhelming superiority in numbers, but our soldiers have to wait until they are shot at before they can fire. He said that our military is fighting people who have infiltrated from Syria and Iran.

His unit is stationed right in the middle of the Sunni Triangle. "These people have been fighting each other for three thousand years. We're not going to get out of there anytime soon." It was obvious in talking to the soldiers that they are frustrated because we have to fight on the enemy's terms. That's a classic case of asymmetric warfare.

Today's asymmetric warfare comes in many varieties: hit-and-run attacks, suicide bombings, guerrilla warfare, kidnapping, disinformation, and much more. Terrorists operate in small, loosely organized cells that spread across many nations. Some are "sleeper cells" that spring into action after years of dormancy. Michael Novak says,

> *Osama bin Laden has grasped the vulnerabilities of free and open societies today. Their technological networks are very complex, highly integrated, and easy to disrupt with precise acts of violence. Tall buildings like the skyscrapers of New York are manifestly vulnerable. The same is true of great suspension bridges, nuclear power plants, water reservoirs, communications hubs, even the virus-prone internet.* [2]

Novak goes on to say that Osama bin Laden "demonstrated how relatively easy it is for a small, disciplined, highly trained cadre of warriors willing to die in the attempt to wreak horrific damage, and to terrorize entire nations."

THE ENEMY'S GOAL: DIVIDE AND DISCOURAGE

In all of this, it helps to remember that the goal of the lesser power is not to utterly defeat the larger power. Instead, the lesser power intends to harass the larger power until, wearied by an opponent he cannot seem to find, the greater power gives up the struggle. Time in that sense is on the side of the lesser power. Few of us have the stomach for a war that never seems to end. If the lesser power can divide and dishearten the greater power, the lesser power can win even though he is badly outnumbered. One writer summarized the matter this way: "The ideal war is one that no one realizes war is being waged, that is mostly invisible, not because its actions are camouflaged, but because they look like something else. War need never be declared again because we are always at war."[3]

"We are always at war." You could hardly find a better statement to describe the Christian life. Satan is the ultimate terrorist who led the first rebellion in the history of the universe. His attempt to unseat God was the first insurgency. Though he never had a chance of succeeding, he continues to fight against God. Think of how the Bible describes him:

He is a cunning deceiver (2 Cor. 11:3).

He is the adversary (1 Peter 5:8).

He is the "father of all lies" (John 8:44).

He is the slanderer (Rev. 13:6).

He is the tempter (Matt. 4:3).

He is the destroyer (Rev. 9:11).

He is the thief who comes to kill and destroy (John 10:10).

He is a murderer (John 8:44).

He is the serpent (Gen. 3:1; Rev. 12:9).

He is the dragon (Rev. 12:7).

He is the "evil one" (Matt. 13:19).

He is the "accuser of [the] brothers" (Rev. 12:10).

He accuses us day and night before the Lord (Zech. 3:1).

He is ruler of the darkness of the world (Eph. 6:12).

He blinds the minds of unbelievers (2 Cor. 4:4).

He is the prince of the power of the air (Eph. 2:2).

He is the prince of this world (John 12:31).

He is the god of this world (2 Cor. 4:4).

He is the lawless one (2 Thess. 2:8–9).

He masquerades as an angel of light (2 Cor. 11:14).

He roams the earth looking for someone to devour (1 Peter 5:8).

He hatches clever schemes in order to outwit us (2 Cor. 2:11).

We can see something of his basic nature in the five "I wills" of Isaiah 14:13–14: "*I will* ascend to heaven; *I will* raise my throne above the stars of God; *I will* sit enthroned on the mount of assembly, on the utmost heights of the sacred mountain. *I will* ascend above the tops of the clouds; *I will* make myself like the Most High" (italics added).

Satan thought he could lead a rebellion that could dethrone God Himself. Evidently a multitude of angels followed him in his desperate insurgency against the Creator. Not only did he fail utterly; he and his followers were cast out of heaven. Since then he has spearheaded an unending war against God that has spread across the universe. Though originally a creature of unimaginable beauty ("O morning star, son of the dawn," v. 12), having been cast down to the earth, he became the epitome of darkness itself.

There is no truth in him. There is no goodness in him. There is no reverence in him. There is no kindness in him. There is no love in him. There is no justice in him. He is evil through and through.

He opposes God with every fiber of his being. He hates the right and promotes the wrong. He lies and cheats and deceives. He disguises himself in order to capture his prey. He attacks all of God's children, all the time, everywhere, by all means possible. He stops at nothing to steal, kill, and destroy. He is a master counterfeiter. He is the ultimate terrorist.

He doesn't fight fair.

THE ENEMY'S WEAKNESS

But there is another side of the story. Though he is far stronger than any human, he is not stronger than God. It is precisely at this point that many Christians go astray, attributing to Satan power that belongs to God alone. He exists only because God allows him to exist. If God willed it, Satan would be destroyed in an instant.

In Job 1 Satan must ask permission to afflict Job. Jesus told Peter in Luke 22:31 that Satan asked (God for permission) to sift him like wheat—a reference to Peter's denial of Christ. That thought may shock you because it is sometimes said that Satan has no authority over the Christian. That's true in one sense, because we know Satan can do nothing without God's express permission. Erwin Lutzer summarizes the truth this way:

> *The devil is just as much God's servant in his rebellion as he was God's servant in the days of his sweet obedience. Even today, he cannot act without God's express permission; he can neither tempt, coerce, demonize, nor make so much as a single plan without the consent and approval of God. We can't quote Luther too often: The devil is God's devil!*[4]

He is powerful but not omnipotent. He is smart but not omniscient. He can travel the universe but he is not omnipresent.

Before his rebellion, Satan was the shining epitome of God's creation. Afterward, he was and is the epitome of evil itself. In one foolish moment of unprecedented arrogance, he gave up his position as God's prime minister to become the leader of the universal forces of darkness.

His rebellion utterly failed. He was decisively defeated at the cross of Christ. And yet he fights on, in a war he is bound to lose.

Having said all of this, one important question remains to be answered: If Christ defeated Satan, why is there so much evil in the world? In the words of a popular Christian book, Satan is alive and well on Planet Earth. He doesn't look very defeated to me. Certainly the devil seems to be having his way. How else can you explain a woman suffocating her own children? Or high school students going on shooting rampages? How do you explain evil in the high places, Satanism on the rise, and a river of pornographic filth flowing over the Internet?

He's Out on Bail

The New Testament presents the truth about the devil in two different ways. On one hand, we are told over and over again that at the cross Satan was defeated as completely as anyone can be defeated. On the other hand, we are warned about the devil who roams about as a roaring lion, seeking someone to devour (1 Peter 5:8). And we are told to put on the armor of God so we can stand in the evil day (Eph. 6:10–17). Is this not a contradiction?

I think the answer is no, but we need to do some careful thinking at this point. What happened at the cross was indeed the total defeat of Satan. In legal terms he was tried, found guilty, and sentenced to ultimate, eternal destruction. That sentence has not yet been executed, but there is no way for Satan to escape it. (Lo! His doom is sure.) Until the day when he will be cast into the lake of fire once and for all, he is destroying lives, breaking up homes, and disrupting God's work as much as he can.[5]

If you prefer a military analogy, the cross was D-day in World War II. Once the Allies came ashore in Normandy, the German defeat was certain. Although much fighting ensued, and many soldiers died, the Allies won the war on December 6, 1944. Satan's D-day happened when Christ died on the cross. Since then his defeat has been certain, his ultimate surrender guaranteed. Meanwhile, he fights on in his desperate battle, a defeated but still dangerous foe.

He's Outnumbered

There is no better picture of Satan's strategy than the modern concept of asymmetric warfare. Though heavily outnumbered by the armies of the Lord, and having lost his personal battle with God, he now uses unconventional warfare to bring down the Lord's people. Satan rarely attacks us head-on, because we are ready for such things. But he comes at us from unusual angles, playing on our minds, slowing us down, throwing one roadblock after another in our way, dividing us from one another and from the Lord, causing us to doubt and then to fear and finally to give in to discouragement.

There are seasons in life for all of us when nothing comes easy. Even the tiniest routines of life don't work as well as they ought to. The dishwasher breaks, the car won't start, our expenses mount up, a project at work misfires, a cherished friend grows distant, our children frustrate us, and our spouse seems impatient and uncaring. In those moments we are facing true asymmetric spiritual warfare because we are being hit in many places at once. As things pile up, it becomes increasingly difficult to maintain our spiritual equilibrium.

THE ENEMY DOESN'T FIGHT FAIR

Most of your spiritual battles will not present you with enormous, life-changing choices, or at least they won't seem that way at the time. Either you get angry or you don't. You stay up late to finish your homework, or you make up a creative excuse. When you visit the department store you pay cash, or you break your promise not to use your credit card. You repeat the unkind story you heard, or you decide to keep it to yourself. You pass by the magazine rack in the airport terminal, or you stop and begin to browse. You get up early to exercise, or you roll over for another thirty minutes of sleep.

No one will know whether you exercised or not. No one will know (at least not till the end of the month) if you used your credit card. And no one will know (unless you are audited) whether you lied on your tax return. God has ordained that our spiritual progress should be measured not by huge battles won or lost, but by a thousand daily skirmishes no one else knows about.

You wouldn't commit adultery, but you don't mind looking at certain Internet sites. You wouldn't lie, but you do make excuses. You wouldn't steal, but you use your credit card foolishly. You wouldn't deliberately hurt someone, but you do pass along gossip because it seems harmless. The whole point of asymmetric warfare (from Satan's point of view) is to discourage us to the point that we feel hopeless about our own spiritual progress. When that happens, he has won the battle even though all the resources of heaven are on our side.

In thinking about spiritual warfare from this perspective, keep two things in mind:

(1) Satan's goal is to discourage you so that you feel like giving up, and you quit trusting Christ.

(2) Satan doesn't fight fair.

He does not observe the traditional rules of warfare. He uses anything and everything that he can to bring us down. This is part of what Paul meant when he spoke about "the devil's schemes" in Ephesians 6:11. The word *schemes* might also be translated as "traps" or "tricks" or "tactics." A Texas politician was asked why a certain candidate had lost an election. "It happened because he forgot the first rule of knife fighting: There are no rules."

Satan doesn't fight fair. He's not going to give you an even break. He is a liar, a deceiver, a diabolical "angel of light" who comes to you in a thousand guises, tempting you to disobey the Lord. And he's a lot smarter than you are. He knows your weak points better than you do. Because he is invisible, he can attack you any time of the day or night. And because he has hosts of subordinates, he can pick a lot of battles at once.

How can we fight back against the devil as he wages asymmetric warfare against us? Here are four practical suggestions.

Adopt a Warfare Mentality

The idea of Christians standing clothed in full armor has captured the mind and heart of every generation. All mature believers understand that they are called to fight—to put on their armor, to take up their weapons of righteousness, to stand against the fierce assault of evil and, having done all, to stand victorious at the end of the day.

Adopting a warfare mentality means understanding that we are always at war, that a battle is raging all around us, and that we ourselves are frontline soldiers. In the old days soldiers saw the enemy. A common battleground rule was "Don't fire until you see the whites of their eyes." But in modern warfare you rarely see the enemy. In the spiritual battle, we fight a foe that is invisible to us, and for that reason it is easy to forget that we are in a battle at all until the attack suddenly comes.

Raise the Spiritual Alert Level

Since 9/11 those of us living in the United States have become very familiar with the color-coded terror alert system. After every threat, the level is raised and then eventually lowered. The problem with the constant raising and lowering is that people stop taking the alerts seriously. They think, *We must be safe since there haven't been any more major attacks on American soil.* That sort of thinking plays into the hands of the terrorists because it leads eventually to complacency. In a sense, time is on their side. We have to be right every time in order to be safe. The terrorists only have to be right once. Mao Tse-tung remarked that the guerrilla "swims like a fish in the sea of the people." The suicide bomber seems like just a traveler until he detonates himself.

The same thing is true in the spiritual realm. We're not safe just because we think we are. Anything can become a weapon. Just as a natural gas pipeline can become a weapon of mass destruction, so in the spiritual battle, our careless habits or our relationships can be what Satan uses to take us out.

The ancient Chinese philosopher Sun Tzu wrote a classic treatise called *The Art of War*. In it he advised warriors never to go to battle unless the battle was already won in the mind of the enemy. Overconfidence leads us to many crushing mistakes, something Peter found out the hard way when he denied Christ less than five hours after he had pledged his loyalty (Luke 22:31–34).

Beware of thinking that you have conquered some sin or that you are beyond certain temptations. Red flag! You never know what you might do under pressure. According to J. C. Ryle, the great Anglican theologian, "He who would make great strides in holiness must first consider the greatness of sin." Anselm of Canterbury famously remarked, "You have not yet considered the gravity of sin." Scottish Presbyterian Robert Murray McCheyne said it even more pointedly, "I have begun to realize that the seeds of every known sin still linger in my heart."

This is a point of great spiritual advance. Beware of spiritual presumption. The traditional reading of 1 Corinthians 10:12 offers this warning: "Therefore let him who thinks he stands take heed lest he fall" (NKJV). Here is a more colorful rendering of the same verse: "Don't be so naive and self-confident. You're not exempt. You could fall flat on your face as easily as anyone else. Forget about self-confidence; it's useless. Cultivate God-confidence" (THE MESSAGE).

Renounce the Devil and Confess Christ Openly

Perhaps this is part of what Christ meant when He promised that whoever confesses Him openly, He will acknowledge before the Father in heaven, and whoever denies Him, He will deny before the Father (Matt. 10:32–33). In the early days of the Christian church, baptismal candidates were asked, "Do you renounce the devil and all his works?" That same question is still asked today in many churches before a believer is baptized. It is entirely biblical, and we should ask it of ourselves on a daily basis. While I do not believe in praying to the devil or "rebuking the devil" verbally (that is better left to the Lord Jesus Christ, in my opinion), I do believe it is entirely proper that when we pray we should renounce the devil and pray for God's help. Is this not what we mean when we pray, "Lead us not into temptation, but deliver us from the evil one" (Matt. 6:13)?

Michael Green wrote, "It cannot be emphasized too much that the only name which brings fear to Satan is the name of Jesus, and the only place that makes him give way is Calvary. There is power in the blood of Jesus. There is nothing like it in all the world."[6]

Often we wonder if God will take us back after we have sinned. The answer is yes, He'll take you back, but you'll never know until you make that journey on your own. While hosting a question-and-answer program on a national radio broadcast, I took one final call before going off the air. As soon as I heard the man's voice, I knew he was distraught. He proceeded to tell me a story unlike anything I have ever heard before. "I used to be a Christian but my wife left me for another man. When she told me she was leaving, I got angry and ripped up the Bible in front of her. Then I denied God in the name of the Trinity." His voice broke and he started weeping. "I know it was wrong to do that, but I don't think God will ever take me back. What can I do?"

I glanced at the clock and saw that we had about ninety seconds left in the program. This was the kind of call I wished we had a whole hour to discuss. But the seconds were ticking away, and I had to say something quickly. "Sir, I don't have much time, so let me tell you this one thing. I know God loves you just the way you are, and He will take you back."

"But I ripped up the Bible in front of my wife."

"Sir, I know God loves you, and He will take you back."

"But I denied God in the name of the Trinity."

"God loves you and He will take you back." The man wept

openly as I said those words. Now we were down to the last thirty seconds. "We're almost out of time, so I want you to listen carefully. Your broken heart tells me that God will take you back. The Lord never turns away a broken heart. When this program is over, I want you to get on your knees, put the Bible in front of you, tell the Lord you know the Bible is the Word of God, and ask Him to forgive you. And I want you to renounce your denial of faith. Tell the Lord that you know He is God, and ask the Lord Jesus to forgive you. Ask Him for a fresh start. If you do that, you will not be turned away."

With that, our time ran out and the program was over. I never heard from the man again. I don't know if he took my counsel or not. But I am sure I told him the truth. No matter how great our sin may be, if we turn to the Lord, He will abundantly pardon. "Who is a God like you, who pardons sin and forgives the transgression of the remnant of his inheritance? You do not stay angry forever but delight to show mercy" (Micah 7:18).

Settle In for the Long Haul

This may be the most important principle of all. Shortly after 9/11, the president told us that the war against terror would not be won easily or quickly. It would take years of determination and the willingness to endure setbacks and further attacks. Perhaps it will never totally be won. There aren't many final victories in asymmetric warfare.

In the spiritual realm, we are told that our enemies cannot ultimately defeat us. But they can discourage us so much that we put down our weapons and leave the battlefield. Satan is a defeated foe, yet he is also a roaring lion (1 Peter 5:8). Because we are joined to Jesus Christ, Satan cannot finally defeat us, and eventually he himself will be vanquished once and for all. But that day has not yet come. Between now and then we will see more battles, more struggles, some bitter defeats, and some stupendous victories. But mostly the spiritual struggle will rage on a thousand fronts at once. Therefore, we must not be surprised at sudden attacks, discouraging events, personal disappointments, financial setbacks, friends who let us down, or days when nothing seems to go right.

All of this is part and parcel of asymmetric spiritual warfare. That does not mean that everything bad that happens to us is caused by Satan directly. But it is certainly true that Satan uses all the adversities of life to discourage us and to tempt us to turn away from the Lord.

I personally am skeptical of any theory of the spiritual life that promises victory without struggle. If you think about it, victory without struggle is self-contradictory. Victory implies a triumph reached in the face of unrelenting difficulties. Football coaches like to say, "No pain, no gain," and that is equally true of the spiritual life.

ONE LITTLE WORD

Martin Luther understood the concept of asymmetric spiritual warfare, even though he probably never heard the term. Think about these famous words from the hymn "A Mighty Fortress":

And though this world, with devils filled, should threaten to undo us,
We will not fear, for God hath willed His truth to triumph through us:
The Prince of Darkness grim, we tremble not for him;
His rage we can endure, for lo, his doom is sure,
One little word shall fell him.

We are attacked on every side by spiritual forces that strike us in our weak points and come to us in unexpected ways. Though they cannot utterly defeat us, they can wear us down until we feel like giving up. The power of Christ is more than enough to defeat the devil, but victory will not come easily or without a heavy cost.

When faced with temptation, we must take the "way of escape" God provides for us (1 Cor. 10:13 NKJV). We are to flee sinful situations (2 Tim. 2:22), confess Christ openly (Matt. 10:32; Hebrews 10:23; Rev. 12:11), put to death the deeds of the flesh

(Rom. 8:13), yield our bodies to God (Rom. 12:1–2), rely on the power of the Holy Spirit (Gal. 5:16), and choose the path of costly obedience (Luke 9:57–62).

Luther says that when we face the devil, "one little word" will fell him. Jesus is that "one little word." The cross proved that our Lord is the victor over the devil for time and eternity. We are in a battle whose outcome has been determined since the beginning of the universe.

From our standpoint we fight against an enemy who attacks without warning. Sometimes we fall under his crushing blows. More often we are hit with dozens of glancing blows one after another. We stumble in the battle, not from direct hits or large mortar fire, but from strategically placed boulders.

But if Jesus has defeated the devil, why does the devil so often defeat us? In order to understand Satan's strategy of asymmetric warfare, let's go back to the beginning of the Bible, to a paradise called Eden.

It all began with a talking snake.

SNAKE EYES

"The greatest trick the devil ever pulled was convincing the world he doesn't exist."

—CHARLES BAUDELAIRE

THE BIBLE MAKES NO SENSE UNLESS we understand the first few chapters of Genesis. These chapters answer a crucial question: Where did we come from, and how did we get from where we started to where we are today? The way that question is worded assumes that somewhere along the way, a massive change occurred in the universe. Genesis 1 tells us that when God finished with creation, He declared it "very good." On that day there was no crime, no poverty, no sickness, and no death. There were no broken homes, no latchkey children, no abusive husbands, no drug pushers, no murderers, and no child molesters. What God created was perfect, and pristine in its beauty. The whole earth was a place of peace and tranquility. In short, the world as it came from the hand of God was paradise.

Obviously something has gone wrong with that world, because evil is found in abundance today. Now the roses have thorns, and we have made bombs powerful enough to kill ten or twenty million people at a time. What happened to the paradise God created? The Bible answers that question with the little word *sin*. Sin has come into the world, and nothing has worked right since.

STUDYING THE ENEMY'S TACTICS

The Bible does not tell us everything we might like to know about sin. For example, we are not told clearly where sin came from in the beginning. The serpent suddenly shows up in Genesis 3 with no introduction at all. He's simply there, in the garden, going about his diabolical work.

As we approach our text, it's useful to keep two things in mind. First, this is history, not myth or legend or saga or poetry. There really was a serpent that really could talk. There really was a woman named Eve, who really ate the fruit and gave some to Adam, who also ate. And that is the true account of the first temptation and the first human sin.

Second, this story also teaches us an important truth about how the devil tempts us today. Though these events took place thousands of years ago, they have an amazing relevance to the twenty-first century. We ought to study this story of the first temptation in the same way that a general studies his enemy. Before committing his force to battle, a good leader studies his opponent carefully. Where does he like to attack? How? When? How often? And under what conditions? If you go into battle armed with that information, your chances of victory are much stronger. Reading Genesis 3 is like reading the devil's playbook. Let's look carefully at the story of the first temptation and watch as the various acts unfold before us.

Act 1: The Approach Is Subtle and Unexpected

"Now the serpent was more crafty than any of the wild animals the LORD God had made" (Gen. 3:1a).

Some things we know and some things we don't know about this story. We know that the serpent is the devil (see Rev. 12:9). But how did the devil gain entry into paradise? How could a serpent talk? And while we're on the subject, does that mean all the animals could talk before the fall? The answer to all those questions is the same: I don't know. The Bible simply doesn't give us enough information to answer those questions with certainty. Evidently they don't matter or God would have told us.

I think it's clear from what follows that Eve has no idea what is about to happen. Why should she? She's quite literally in paradise. It's not as if she got up that day and thought to herself, *I'd better have my quiet time today because a talking serpent is going to tempt me to sin. If I give in, I'll bring heartache, misery, sadness, despair, loneliness, trouble, murder, mayhem, hatred, and every form of evil to billions of people for thousands of years to come.* No, it wasn't like that at all. She wasn't expecting to encounter a talking serpent or to be tempted to commit the first sin. She wasn't looking for the serpent, but the serpent was definitely looking for her.

In my mind's eye I picture her walking along the banks of the river that ran through the garden of Eden. It's a sunny day and she enjoys the breeze blowing through her hair and the soft feel of fresh grass beneath her feet. The flowers are in full bloom and she can hear the birds calling to each other from the trees of the forest. It is the sort of day that we all dream about, a perfect day in paradise.

Then she spots the serpent. She doesn't recoil in fear. Why should she? What is there to fear in paradise? The creature before her is stunningly beautiful. When he speaks, his voice is captivating.

If temptation gave us a warning call, we'd be much better prepared. The fact that the serpent shows up in paradise leads me to this suggestion: When everything is going well in your life, beware! You are a prime candidate for satanic attack. Our instincts tell us that temptation tends to come when we are down on our luck, and sometimes it happens that way. But we are just as likely to be tempted when our bills are paid, our job is going well, the boss likes us, our spouse loves us, our children are reasonably well behaved, the folks at church are glad to see us, and the doctor says we are in perfect health. Be warned. When the good times roll, our guard is down and we are prime candidates for the "fiery darts" of the devil.

Act 2: The Strategy Involves Conversation and Controversy

"He said to the woman, 'Did God really say, "You must not eat from any tree in the garden"?' The woman said to the serpent, 'We may eat fruit from the trees in the garden, but God did say, "You must not eat fruit from the tree that is in the middle of the garden, and you must not touch it, or you will die"'" (Gen. 3:1b–3).

The serpent's first move is brilliant. In essence, he challenges Eve to a game of Bible Trivia. What happens next is a three-part conversation in which the serpent speaks, Eve responds, and the serpent speaks again. The whole exchange could have been over in less than a minute. The serpent's Bible Trivia question is this: "Did God really say, 'You must not eat from any tree in the garden'?" That's a clever query. After all, Eve was not present when God spoke to Adam. She had to rely on her husband's explanation. The question itself turns on the word *really*. One translation even begins with that word: "Really? Did God really say . . ."

The question boils down to this: How well does Eve know the Word of God? As we shall see, she knows it pretty well, but not well enough. Because she has a general idea of what God said but is hazy on the details, the serpent will pounce on her lack of specific knowledge.

In her response Eve makes three mistakes. First, she downplays the permission. God had said they could eat from *any* tree of the garden (Gen. 2:16). Eve lessens the impact of God's permission from "any tree" to "the trees," a subtle but important shift in emphasis. Second, she added to the prohibition. God had forbidden them to eat from the Tree of the Knowledge of Good and Evil. But Eve added the phrase, "You must not touch it." Finally, she downplayed the judgment for disobedience. God had said, "You will surely die," while Eve says, "You will die." Again, this is a subtle difference.

Eve had to get her information from Adam, which means that Adam incorrectly relayed what God had said, Eve misunderstood it, or perhaps she changed it on her own. In a sense, Eve's "paraphrase" of God's Word in and of itself is not especially objectionable. She is close to the truth. She is quoting God's Word, sort of. And where did that part about not touching the tree come from? Perhaps Adam suggested it as a logical way to stay out of trouble. If so, he was simply being a wise husband and showing proper care for his wife. But if Adam said, "God said, 'Don't touch the tree,'" then Adam was adding to God's Word. And if Eve interpreted it that way, she was adding to God's Word. Either way, the net effect is to make God sound more restrictive than He really is.

But there is a greater point that must not be missed. *If you are going to talk to the devil, make sure you quote God's Word accurately.* When we are tempted, we will never be delivered by a "general" knowledge of the Word. It won't help us to "sort of" know the truth. We must know and stand upon what God has actually said.

So why did Eve get in trouble? First, she didn't know the truth of the Word of God. Second, she shouldn't have been discussing God's Word with the serpent. Third, she should have asked Adam to help her in this situation instead of going it alone. Those who think they are an equal match for the devil will soon find out they were sadly mistaken.

When you are tempted, don't stop to talk it over. When Potiphar's wife is pulling you down into the bed, don't stop to pray with her. Run for your life! Leave your jacket and run for safety. Don't negotiate with the devil. And don't talk it over with his representatives. Remember that his representative could be your best friend or a family member, a coworker, or someone else you know very well. The devil sometimes uses those we love in order to lead us astray. Your best defense against temptation will always be an accurate knowledge of the Word. Know it. Read it. Memorize it. Quote it when the devil knocks at your door.

Act 3: The Conversation Leads to Doubt and Desire

"'You will not surely die,' the serpent said to the woman. 'For God knows that when you eat of it your eyes will be opened, and you will be like God, knowing good and evil.' When the woman saw that the fruit of the tree was good for food and pleasing to the eye, and also desirable for gaining wisdom, she took some and ate it" (Gen. 3:4–6a).

At this point the serpent openly denies what God has said. In the Hebrew the expression is very strong. Literally it reads, "Not, you shall surely die." The serpent took the very phrase God used and put the word *not* in front of it. That's why you'd better know your Bible before you start arguing with Satan. He's not only smarter than you; he knows God's Word through and through. He just doesn't believe it.

The first doctrine that the devil denies is God's judgment. God said, "You will certainly die." Satan said, "You will not certainly die." Why did he deny this doctrine and not something like the existence of God? The answer is simple: *If you are convinced that you can get away with sin, sooner or later you're going to do it.* If you think that no one will know, no one will notice, no one will ever call you to account for your actions, you'll eventually give in. Why not commit adultery if you think you can get away with it? Why not steal or kill or cheat? If there are no consequences for sin, then there is no judge and no authority, and no reason not to indulge your wild desires.

Then the serpent questions God's goodness. He implies that God is holding back something from Eve that would make her happy. "You will be like God." What an incentive that is. Why not? Who wouldn't want to "be like God"? The serpent's words were designed to cause Eve to feel deprived and cheated by God.

The downward spiral has started. First, Eve listened when she shouldn't have listened. She talked when she shouldn't have talked.

She thought about what the devil said when she should have ignored it. Now she is about to fall right into his trap.

Her response reveals how clever the devil is. He's got her on three different levels (see 1 John 2:16).

(1) **The Practical Level.** The fruit was good to eat. That's the lust of the flesh.

(2) **The Emotional Level.** It looked beautiful to her. That's the lust of the eyes.

(3) **The Spiritual Level.** It would make her wise. That's the pride of life.

The devil has now got her hook, line, and sinker. She's already a goner and she doesn't even know it. I'm sure the fruit did look good. She probably took it in her hands, felt it, and even enjoyed the pleasant fragrance. But please remember this: When you start fondling forbidden fruit, you're already in the pit. You've committed the sin in your heart long before you take that first bite. If you don't want to get trapped, don't stop to inspect the fruit. Don't spend time thinking about how nice it would be, how good it would taste, or how much you deserve it.

We play this game so many ways. "I know God says adultery is wrong, but I really do love him and God wants me to be happy." "I know God says He hates divorce, but my marriage is the pits." "I know God calls me to purity, but I'm single and so lonely." "I know God says stealing is wrong, but everyone else does it. Why can't I?" On and on we go, offering one rationalization after another. Mark it down. When you start saying, "I know what God says, but I think He'll make an exception for me," you are on the verge of spiritual disaster.

There are several crucial lessons here:

(1) When we doubt God's goodness, sin won't seem so sinful.

(2) Satan wants us to feel deprived by God.

(3) We can always justify disobedience if we try hard enough.

Self-pity is a dangerous emotion that leads to many wrong decisions. A friend wrote in an e-mail that she was going through a particularly bad day. She realized that she was wallowing in a sea of self-pity, and she knew from experience that she had to get out of it quickly. From her days in Alcoholics Anonymous she knew how dangerous those "pity parties" can be: "This is when drinkers drink. This is when smokers smoke. This is when eaters eat. This is when gamblers gamble." And, I would add, this is when cheaters cheat, liars lie, angry people lose their temper, and adulterers commit adultery. You will never grow spiritually as long as you listen to the devil's lie that says, "Go ahead. You deserve it. It won't matter. You've been cheated in life and now it's time to live a little." If you listen carefully, you can hear the hiss of hell in those evil words.

The downward spiral is almost complete. First, you talk with the devil. Second, you believe the devil. Third, you obey the devil. And fourth, you are conquered by the devil. Truly, there is nothing new under the sun. What the serpent did to Eve, he still does today—because the strategy still works.

Act 4: The Result Is Collaboration and Catastrophe

"She also gave some to her husband, who was with her, and he ate it. Then the eyes of both of them were opened, and they realized they were naked; so they sewed fig leaves together and made coverings for themselves" (Gen. 3:6b–7).

The end comes very quickly. Notice the verbs in verse 6: saw . . . took . . . gave . . . ate. Evidently Eve doesn't hesitate, and neither does Adam. Eve has now joined the serpent's team. By giving the fruit to Adam, she is doing the serpent's dirty work for him, and she is dragging her husband down with her. But that's what happens when we yield to temptation. We never fall alone; others are always hurt by our rebellion and disobedience. We stand together, we fall together, and in the end, we suffer together.

Notice how ordinary the first sin is. It's just a bite of fruit.

Nothing special about it. The first sin was not murder or some terrible sexual sin. No, it's something very ordinary, something we all have done, just taking a bite of fruit. And I can imagine that when she ate the fruit, Eve said to herself, "This is really good." And perhaps she said to Adam, "Honey, have a bite. I touched it and nothing happened to me. This is the best fruit I've ever had."

And by the way, where was Adam when all this was going down? The text says he was "with her." That sounds like he was standing right by her side while she was talking to the serpent. What a total doofus! Maybe he was grinning to himself and enjoying the intellectual sparring that took place between the serpent and his wife. Perhaps he thought it was just some cute parlor game. If Adam had been a true spiritual leader, he would have taken a hoe and hacked off the serpent's head. The world would have been a better place if he had taken leadership.

First Timothy 2:14 draws an important conclusion from this verse: "And Adam was not the one deceived; it was the woman who was deceived and became a sinner." Eve was tricked by the devil. Perhaps he came to her because he knew he could appeal to her emotions. But Adam was not deceived. He had heard the original command from God, and he knew it was wrong to eat the fruit. He wasn't tricked at all. And as the head of his family (and the "federal head" of the whole human race), he is held morally culpable for the first sin.

It wasn't Eve's fault. She sinned first, but Adam is to blame. That's why Romans 5 says that sin entered through Adam. He should have known better, he should have exercised leadership to protect his wife, and he should have killed the serpent when he had the chance. But he didn't. And the rest is history. Men, learn this lesson: When you fail to exercise spiritual leadership, your wife and your children will always pay the price.

Eve never dreamed what would happen next. She truly thought that she would gain enlightenment. But her eyes were opened and she suddenly knew she was naked. And Adam's eyes were opened and he knew he was naked. Innocence was gone forever. Now the full impact of their disobedience begins to hit home. Now they are ashamed to see each other naked. Quickly they make a pitiful covering of fig leaves. But sinners can never adequately cover up their own sin. The fig leaves keep falling off. And you can never replace them fast enough.

LITTLE STEPS IN THE WRONG DIRECTION

How did Adam and Eve end up like this? It was a series of little steps in the wrong direction. But all those small steps added up to one huge catastrophe that still haunts the world today.

From the standpoint of thousands of years later, we see Satan's strategy clearly. When he came to Eve he began with an "innocent" question. Little by little, he led her to the place where she was willing to do what she had previously never even dreamed of doing. He even co-opted her onto his team so she was doing his work for him. The devil uses that same strategy today because it still works. And notice his ultimate lie. He said, "God knows . . . you will know." He took a truth and twisted it violently. When they sinned, their eyes were opened and they truly did know evil—on a personal basis. But the wisdom they sought could never be found through rebellion. The enlightenment they dreamed of turned out to be deep moral darkness. No wonder they were ashamed.

Satan promised liberation through rebellion. What they got was slavery, sin, shame, and death. Let us learn one overarching truth from this passage: *Every temptation is a lie wrapped in a promise of freedom.* Satan is the Father of Lies. He lies consistently. He lies because it is his nature to lie. He is the first and greatest deceiver. All Satan's apples have worms.

What really happened that day in the garden of Eden? Theologians call it "the fall." They mean that Adam and Eve fell from a state of innocence into a state of sin, shame, slavery, and death. And what they did has been passed down across the generations so that all of us inherit a nature that causes us to rebel against God. That day in Eden, man declared his independence from God. As a result, all of us are born with a clenched fist daring God to tell us what to do. Human nature is now thoroughly corrupt. All are sinners. We are born that way, we live that way, and we will die that way. Sin is now the environment in which we breathe. Every relationship is corrupted because sin always separates us from each other and from God.

Who's Going to Be God Today?

Satan gives people what they want so that they will eventually get what he wants them to have. And he never shows us the consequences of sin. We can never undo that wrong decision, even though we may repent heartily. We have to discover that on our own, when it is too late to do anything about the decision. The serpent repeated the lie that now rules the world: Man can be like God. This was the original sin, and it is at the heart of every bad choice you've ever made.

At this point we are faced with a decision that each of us must make every single day. It goes something like this. We can reject God's sovereignty and decide to fight against it. But that rebellion leads inevitably to anger, bitterness, despair, and finally to a hardened heart.

I know a few believers who have chosen this path. Some end up dropping out of church altogether because they are so angry they cannot come to worship anymore. In my experience, however, most of the people who choose this path stay in church and end up as very angry Christians. They are hard to talk to because they are secretly (or not so secretly) fighting against the Lord. Usually they have suffered an enormous personal loss and cannot find a way to reconcile what they lost with the God they have always worshiped. So they come to church Sunday after Sunday, sitting in the pews, singing the hymns, praying the prayers, going through the motions; but their hearts are not in it because down deep, they are angry at what God has done. They have the "wounded spirit" spoken of in

Proverbs 18:14 (KJV). It is very difficult to help them unless God's Spirit softens their hearts.

We have another choice we can make. If we accept God's sovereignty as true, submit ourselves to God, and acknowledge that He is free to do what He wants to do, that submission leads to joyful praise. It is not that we will praise God directly for the pain and sadness we suffer or for the sinful acts of others. But we will praise God that He is able to work in, with, and through everything that happens—both the good and the bad—to accomplish His will, make us more like Christ, and bring glory to Himself. To say that is to say nothing more than what Romans 8:28 clearly teaches.

So these are our choices with regard to the truth of God's sovereignty: rejection and anger or submission and praise.

One Saturday night a few years ago I was working in my office at home. I rarely have visitors to my home office, and no one ever drops by on Saturday night. But on this particular night, I heard a knock at the door. When I opened it, there stood an old friend with tears streaming down his face. As he walked in and sat down, he kept repeating two words: "It's over."

I knew what he meant. His marriage was coming to a very sad end. Although both he and his wife were Christians, a series of sinful choices had brought their marriage to a total collapse. That night she told him that she was filing for divorce. My friend sat in my office, tears coursing down his cheeks, thoroughly broken as he realized that soon his marriage would be over and he would be divorced.

He went on to say that two things had sustained him in this agonizing personal crisis. The first one was a song that had been playing on the local Christian station: "Life Is Hard but God Is Good." He had heard it so many times that he knew the words by heart. And he had discovered through his pain that both parts of the title were true. Life *is* hard. No one had to convince him of that. But as he contemplated the wreckage of a marriage he had hoped would last his entire life, he was discovering that even in his pain, God is good.

Then he said that he had learned a verse of Scripture that had helped him greatly. It was Psalm 115:3, "Our God is in heaven; he does whatever pleases him." On the surface, that might seem a strange verse for such a sad moment, yet to him it had been a lifeline. The truth of God's sovereignty and God's freedom meant that what was happening to him was part of the outworking of God's plan. Though human sin had caused it, God had allowed it to come and did not intervene to stop it. Therefore, God would help him through it, and in the end, he would learn many painful and necessary lessons.

That happened a number of years ago. Looking back, my friend would say today that he believes that verse even more than he did then. Nothing happens anywhere in the universe by accident. There is no such thing as luck or fate or chance. God is at work in all things at all times to accomplish His will in the universe. He does whatever pleases Him.

Rebellion Leads to Slavery

I understand why some people rebel against a high view of God's sovereignty. The paradox is this: People who rebel against God usually do so in the name of freedom. They want the freedom to go their own way, follow their own desires, do whatever they want, when they want, with anyone they choose to do it with. Ironically, this sort of "freedom" leads only to slavery. They end up enslaved to sin, chained to addictive behaviors, and locked in the prison house of unrelenting guilt and shame. There is no freedom in rebellion against God. There is only slavery.

But when we submit ourselves to our heavenly Father, when we finally say, "Lord, You are God and I am not," through our tears if necessary, then (and only then) do we discover true freedom. This is what Jesus meant when He said, "You will know the truth, and the truth will set you free" (John 8:32). Those whom the Son sets free are free indeed.

Our basic problem is that we have not acknowledged God's sovereignty over our lives. No wonder we are unhappy and frustrated and unfulfilled. No wonder life doesn't work right. How much better to say with the psalmist, "Come, let us bow down in worship, let us kneel before the LORD our Maker" (Ps. 95:6). There is coming a day when "every knee should bow . . . and every tongue confess that Jesus Christ is Lord, to the glory of God the Father" (Phil. 2:10–11). Why not get a head start and bow your knee and confess that God is God and Jesus Christ is your Lord?

Here is a simple phrase that captures this truth: "The Lord is God and there is no other." I encourage you to say this sentence out loud as a personal affirmation of your own faith.

"MAN NO BE GOD"

Greg and Carolyn Kirschner, who served for many years as missionaries in Jos, Nigeria, wrote about the importance of prayer in the Nigerian culture. They pointed out that the Nigerians seem more naturally aware of God than most Americans do. They saw this sign painted on the side of a bus: "Man no be God." That sums it up, doesn't it? You aren't God, you never were, and you never will be. The sooner we realize that fact, the better off we'll be. And here's the good news. If you really mean it, then you can take a deep breath. Now go and rip that big G off your sweatshirt. You don't have to be God anymore. Let God be God, and all will be well.

Perhaps some of us need to say, "O God, You win. The battle is over. I'm going to stop fighting You." If you need to say that, do it right now. There is abundant joy for those who will admit the most fundamental truth in the universe: He's God and we're not.

Genesis 3 tells us why the human race is so messed up today. There is a direct connection between what happened in the garden that day and the pain, sorrow, sadness, despair, hatred, and rampant evil we see all around us, and the sin we see inside us. We are the way we are because of what Adam and Eve did.

I can sum up the rest of the Bible in one short paragraph. After the fall, God moved to reestablish a relationship with fallen men and women. Thousands of years later He made the ultimate move when His Son, the Lord Jesus Christ, came to earth to die for us. The first sin came from tasting forbidden fruit. The evil of that day would not be overcome until Christ tasted death for all of us on the cross. It took the bloody death of the Son of God to reverse the impact of what happened in Eden.

But we are still only at the beginning of the story. We've seen what can happen when a talking snake pays a visit. Now let's move to a different part of the cosmic battlefield.

It's time to talk about angels and demons.

THREE

WAR IN
HEAVENLY PLACES

"These are times in which a genius would wish to live. It is not in the still calm of life, or the repose of a pacific station, that great characters are formed. The habits of a vigorous mind are formed in contending with difficulties."

—ABIGAIL ADAMS

THIS IS ONE OF THOSE TIMES when the chapter title is important. "War in Heavenly Places" not only describes this chapter; it also tells us what Daniel 10 is all about. This often-overlooked chapter reveals a cosmic struggle between the forces of good and evil. It tells of angels and demons locked in a kind of mortal combat somewhere between heaven and earth. This is like *Star Wars*; only this isn't science fiction. It's real.

In order to get the proper perspective, consider these words by Welsh pastor Geoff Thomas: "Wherever there is a flock of Christ's sheep there are wolves that want to destroy them. Whenever the church advances dark principalities are at work."[1] Whenever the Lord makes an advance into the realm of darkness, the empire of Satan always strikes back. Daniel 10 helps us understand why we encounter delays and difficulties in our service for Christ. It especially helps us understand why our prayers are sometimes hindered and delayed for long seasons, sometimes for many years.

I believe the best way to picture Daniel 10 is to imagine yourself at a play in a majestic theater. As you wait for the program to begin, you can hear noise from behind the curtain, and occasionally the curtain itself is jostled by something or someone hidden from your view. Suddenly the curtain parts for a moment, just for a second, and you can clearly see the action on the stage. Almost before you can focus your eyes, the curtain closes again. You know what you saw, but you wish you had been able to get a better glimpse. That's Daniel 10. Daniel is given a rare insight into things that are normally invisible. It is a view from the seen to the unseen, from the visible to the invisible, from the natural to the supernatural.

THE BACKGROUND OF DANIEL 10

The chapter begins with an important chronological note. Verse 1 tells us that Daniel received his revelation in the third year of Cyrus king of Persia, that is, in 536 B.C. That date is important because that's the year the exile finally ended and the first group of Jews returned to Jerusalem. You may recall that the Jews were taken into captivity for seventy years, and now that time of exile was nearing its end.

Although more than forty-nine thousand people went home that year, Daniel was not among them. Perhaps at his advanced age he could not make the arduous journey. More likely, God simply told him that He had more work in Babylon for him to do. Daniel 10 introduces us to the final vision of the book. Chapter 10 is the prologue, chapter 11 is the vision itself, and chapter 12 gives us the aftermath and the close of the book.

Daniel receives a revelation of the future that involves (1) his people, the nation of Israel, (2) the last days, and (3) a great war (Dan. 10:1). Daniel 11 contains an amazing revelation of Israel's history, culminating in the rise of Antichrist in the final days before the return of Christ. This revelation of a great war that will engulf Israel evidently sent Daniel into mourning. For three weeks he fasted and prayed, eating no food, drinking no wine, and using no lotions (meaning he didn't shower or use deodorant). At the end of the three weeks he was standing by the Tigris River when he saw a most amazing thing:

> *I looked up and there before me was a man dressed in linen, with a belt of the finest gold around his waist. His body was like chrysolite, his face like lightning, his eyes like flaming torches, his arms and legs like the gleam of burnished bronze, and his voice like the sound of a multitude.* (Dan. 10:5–6)

Although this man is not identified, the description sounds very much like the appearance of the Lord Jesus Christ in Revelation 1. And Daniel's response is the same as the apostle John. He fell on his face before this amazing person. I believe that Daniel encountered a preincarnate appearance of the Lord Jesus Christ. The experience was too much for him and he passed out on the ground.

Later a hand touched him and bid him to stand up. I believe the hand belonged not to Jesus but to an angel sent by Him. The angel told Daniel that his prayer had been heard the moment he began praying at the start of his twenty-one-day fast. Why, then, had the answer taken so long to arrive? The angel's explanation is mind-blowing. He said that he had been hindered by demonic opposition between heaven and earth:

> *"Do not be afraid, Daniel. Since the first day that you set your mind to gain understanding and to humble yourself before your God, your words were heard, and I have come in response to them. But the prince of the Persian kingdom resisted me twenty-one days. Then Michael, one of the chief princes, came to help me, because I was detained there with the king of Persia."* (Dan. 10:12–13)

The "prince of the Persian kingdom" cannot be a man, because no man can hinder an angel sent by God. This must be some kind of demonic force assigned by Satan to serve in the court of the Persian king. Evidently his job was to hinder God's work and to discourage God's people in Persia. He must have been a strong demon, because all by himself he stopped an angel cold for twenty-one days. Then Michael (who is an archangel assigned to guard Israel; see Daniel 12:1) intervened, and the angel was able to complete his mission.

At the end of the chapter we get even more information about angelic comings and goings:

> *"Soon I will return to fight against the prince of Persia, and when I go, the prince of Greece will come; but first I will tell you what is written in the Book of Truth. (No one supports me against them except Michael, your prince. And in the first year of Darius the Mede, I took my stand to support and protect him.)"* (Dan. 10:20b–11:1)

This tells us that the angel has left his warfare to come to Daniel and will soon be resuming the heavenly battle. Soon he will fight the "prince of Persia" again and later will take on the "prince of Greece." He also tells Daniel that two years earlier he had somehow interceded to help out Michael (perhaps also fighting against the "prince of Persia").

This is all very mysterious. But if it is to be taken literally, as I think it must be, it tells us of unusual goings-on in the invisible realm where demons and angels duke it out to either promote or obstruct God's work in the world.

If this sounds like a little too much to take, consider the familiar words of Ephesians 6:12: "For our struggle is not against flesh and blood, but against the rulers, against the authorities, against the powers of this dark world and against the spiritual forces of evil in the heavenly realms."

This verse is helpful on several levels. First, it reminds us that *our battle is not against other humans.* Sometimes we focus on the abortionists, the pornographers, the godless politicians, the corrupt business leaders, and the drug dealers as if they were the source of our problems. Yet those people are unwitting dupes of powerful spiritual forces that they know nothing about. They are morally culpable for their choices, yet they are also in the service of evil beings who influence them in ways they do not realize.

Second, this verse teaches us that there are various kinds of demonic powers. There are "rulers," "authorities," "powers of this dark world," and "spiritual forces of evil in the heavenly realms." It's not clear how we should differentiate between them. Perhaps it is enough to know that just as there are various types of angels, the demons are also organized and serve different purposes in Satan's service.

Finally, Ephesians 6:11 encourages us to "put on the full armor of God." Our godly character (or lack of it) actually does make a day-to-day difference. Not only for us, but also in the great struggle between good and evil. We are all foot soldiers in a vast invisible war that stretches across the cosmos.

As I was working on this chapter, I picked up a newsletter that came in the mail yesterday from LoveINC ("Love In the Name of Christ"), headed by Robert Odom, a man whom I know well and admire greatly. LoveINC is doing groundbreaking work in uniting churches to work together to meet the needs of the poor in cities and in depressed rural areas. Robert wrote the lead article, "The Depth of the Call." He recently spoke at an open community meeting in the city of one of his affiliates. During the question-and-answer time, a woman said that 90 percent of the people in that community don't go to church, and asked what they could do about it. Robert replied that he didn't have an answer for the 90 percent. Why, he wondered, aren't the 10 percent living such godly, joyful, selfless, egoless, loving, compassionate lives that the 90 percent are drawn to them and ultimately to Christ? That's a good question.

Robert wrote, "There is no shortage of people talking about Christ, but there is a shortage of people living like Christ." I couldn't get this sentence out of my mind: "When God brings someone out of the deep, not coming out of the deep wiser, more selfless, more committed, more Christlike is dishonoring to God and dishonoring to them and all that they've gone through."[2]

Our godly character really does matter. It matters in our struggle with "principalities and powers," it matters in our Christian walk, and it matters greatly to the watching world. Life is a struggle that will continue till the day we die. There is no release from the battle. If we go AWOL, we simply find a bigger battle on the other side of the hill.

Daniel 10 may seem unusual, but it actually corresponds quite well with the bigger picture presented in the New Testament.

THINGS WE DON'T KNOW FOR CERTAIN

Because this chapter is a peek behind the curtain, it leaves us with many questions we can't answer fully. For instance, what happened during the twenty-one days the angel and the "prince of Persia" were contending together? The text tells us of a conflict but gives no hint as to how the conflict played itself out. We'd also like to know exactly what Michael the archangel did that finally won the day. We can't say with certainty exactly what happened. We can't even conceive of how spirit beings can contend with each other. If we knew the answer, it would probably not make any sense to us.

Geoff Thomas has a helpful word about demonic powers:

The Devil is not omniscient. But though he does not know everything he is highly organised: he has an intricate network. Nothing is left haphazard, even to the smallest detail. Demons are not like dogs let loose in a park, chasing butterflies, sniffing at this bit of grass and at that tree trunk. They plan: they are structured. The Devil's assistants are more cunning than diplomats, and their servants are more beautiful than angels of light.

The Devil has a fifth column and it operates in every area, all the world over. He stirs up prejudice against the church of Christ, always seeking to resist the spread of the gospel and the building of God's kingdom. [3]

As we read a passage like Daniel 10, we'd like to know how our prayers affect heavenly warfare. Some writers suggest that our prayers somehow give strength to weary angels to aid them in their combat. Perhaps that is true. All we can say for certain is that there is a connection between our prayers and the spirit realm. That's what the "wrestling" of Ephesians 6:12 is all about. We wrestle through prayer, obedience to God, and putting on the armor of God. Through these activities we enter the realm of invisible spiritual warfare.

We would like to know if demons and angels are assigned to every nation on earth. We know about Michael and Israel, and the demons assigned to Persia and Greece. Some writers suggest there are angels and demons assigned to every city, town, street, home, school, office, and factory. They make much of "territorial spirits" and the importance of identifying those spirits and praying against them. Outside Daniel 10, no other passage in the Bible tells us about spirit beings assigned to specific nations. We simply don't know how far to take this. It may well be true that there are demons assigned to every street and perhaps to every home, but there is no way to be sure. Evidently it's not an issue we need to understand, or we would be told more about it.

Finally, what about guardian angels? Many people believe that an angel is assigned to each person on earth, or at least to each believer. I think we all may have many guardian angels (cf. Matthew 18:10, which speaks of "their angels"). Some of us need an entire battalion of the heavenly host to watch our backs.

I have mentioned what we don't know (that we wish we knew) in order to bring up an important point. Whenever we read a passage like Daniel 10, it's easy to go off on a tangent. Either we dismiss it as superstition, or we go off the deep end and obsess on the supernatural. Both extremes are wrong. The principle we should follow is this: *The only things we can know for sure about the spiritual realm are those things clearly revealed in the Word of God.* Everything else is speculation. It is important not to go beyond the Scripture at any point with respect to the demonic.

As evangelicals, we believe that the Bible tells us everything we need to know about the spirit world, that everything the Bible says is actually true, and that there is no other authoritative source for information regarding demons and angels. To say that is to say that we take 2 Timothy 3:16 seriously when it says that the Bible is God-breathed and is given to make us thoroughly equipped for teaching, correcting, rebuking, and training in righteousness. Through the written Word of God we have everything we need for life and godliness (2 Peter 1:3–4). Our only authority in the spiritual realm is the Bible itself, not human experience.

Along this line it's important to remember that Daniel wouldn't have known anything about the conflict with the "prince of Persia" if the angel had not told him. It's not as if he was praying for the angels during his fast. "O Lord, help the good angel to fight hard. Lord, please help Michael to hurry up and get in the battle." He didn't know anything about it. He had no knowledge of the supernatural struggle (and had no way of knowing) until the angel revealed it to him.

THINGS WE CAN BE SURE ABOUT

Now let's focus on what we can learn from Daniel 10. Five key statements summarize truth we can use.

God Hears the Prayers of Believers Immediately

The angel told Daniel in Daniel 10:12 that his prayers were heard in heaven the moment he sought wisdom from God. This ought to encourage all of us who wonder if our prayers ever reach beyond the ceiling. The tiniest whisper from a believer on earth is shouted throughout the courts of heaven. God hears us when we pray, and our petitions reach Him the moment they are formed in our hearts. Since there is no time or distance with our heavenly Father, we may pray with the assurance that He hears us as if we were the only ones speaking to Him.

Unseen Spiritual Warfare May Delay Answers to Our Prayers

What happened to Daniel may also happen to us. It may be that answers to our deepest, most heartfelt prayers are sometimes delayed because of "static" coming from the other side of the curtain as angels and demons battle in the invisible realm. I believe this is most likely to happen when we pray about God's cause on the earth. As we enter into serious intercession for unreached people groups, we are likely to encounter many difficulties. And when we pray for our loved ones to be saved and for wayward children to return to the Lord, we should not be surprised that those prayers are not immediately answered. Satan hates that kind of praying because it is a direct attack on his infernal kingdom. He will not give up his captives without a fight.

Wrestling in Prayer Is Exhausting Work

Daniel fasted twenty-one days while he sought the Lord. He fell on his face when he met the Lord Jesus Christ by the Tigris River. Then he bowed down to the ground, totally exhausted, when he heard the angel's explanation.

Daniel started and ended his life serving the Lord. He stood for the truth as a teenager, and now as an old man he battles on. So it will be for all the saints of God. There is no respite from the battle in this life. "This day the noise of battle, the next the victor's song."

My friend Bruce Thorn from Sheffield, Alabama, calls me three or four times a year, and each time it seems as if what he has to say is a message from God to me. In one conversation he shared what God had been saying to him about the need to advance boldly against the devil and his kingdom. Then he said, "Ray, you've got to tell your people that spiritual warfare is serious business." He's right. *This is not war games. This is war!* We are locked in a battle against spiritual forces that are vast beyond all human comprehension. Unless we rely completely on the Lord, we are certain to be defeated.

Colossians 4:2 calls us to be "watchful" when we pray. The word means to "stay awake." This is a call for earnest prayer. It is the opposite of sleepiness or laziness or coldness or indifference. Have you ever noticed how easy it is to be distracted when you pray? Just as you bow your head, the phone rings, your pager beeps, some music distracts you, or you suddenly remember that you have to check the roast in the oven. A thousand things come crowding into your mind. Sometimes it seems as if the devil's best work comes when we decide to pray. He unloads his full armory of distractions against us.

Or perhaps you decide to spend an hour in prayer. So you get on your knees and begin to pray. You pray for yourself, the members of your family, all your friends, the leaders of your church, the missionaries you know, then all the missionaries in the world, then every country in the world. Finally you pray by name for every person in every country of the world (or so it seems). Then you look up and discover you've only been praying for five minutes!

James 5:16 (NKJV) speaks of the "effective, fervent prayers" of the righteous person. They "avail much" with God. They matter to God. He pays attention to "effective, fervent prayers." The Greek word for *fervent* means "boiling." Boiling prayers get God's attention. You'll discover what that means when the doctor says, "We're taking your child away for surgery." Nothing can distract you from prayer then. Praying like this speaks of total concentration. Better a short prayer from the heart than a long prayer that puts you to sleep.

Consider a Marine sentry guarding a base in the Sunni Triangle in central Iraq. Now compare that soldier with a security guard at the local grocery store. Who will be more alert? It had better be the Marine sentry in Iraq. *The one who believes he is on the front lines is going to be more alert.* He has to stay alert because his buddies are depending on him. It's life or death to them.

We mess around in prayer because we think it doesn't matter, when in reality we are sentries standing guard at the front lines of spiritual combat. It's easy to say, "Lord, bless me and my family. And by the way, thank You for this food. Amen." That's good, but it's hardly the kind of prayer that will cause Satan to tremble. It's time for all of us to raise the bar and enter into serious spiritual warfare.

Forces of Good and Evil Are All Around Us

Daniel 10 tells us that behind the movement of men and nations, unseen spiritual forces are at work. No one could have known simply by looking at the Persian court that a great battle was going on between an angel and the "prince of Persia." But when the curtain is pulled back, we see angels and demons battling against each other while human leaders are completely unaware of what is going on. Satan often uses his emissaries to influence government leaders to turn against the people of God. It was true in Persia and in Greece. It is true in Washington, Los Angeles, and Chicago. It is true where you live. Daniel 10 proves conclusively that Satan does not believe in the separation of church and state. He has no problems using his evil minions to harass and hinder the work of God in the world.

But there is another, encouraging side to all of this. Second Kings 6 tells of a time when the mighty army of Syria surrounded the Israelites in a city called Dothan. The situation appeared totally hopeless. When Elisha's servant saw the armies of the enemy on every hand, he despaired and cried out, "What shall we do?" Elisha answered with words that seemed to make no sense, "Those who are with us are more than those who are with them" (vv. 15–16). Then Elisha asked the Lord to open the eyes of his servant. When the servant looked around, he saw above the army of Syria the flaming chariots of the army of God (v. 17). If only we could see beyond the visible. This story in Daniel 10 reminds us that just because we can't see something doesn't mean it isn't there. If for one second we could truly see with the eyes of God, we would behold a vast array of supernatural beings, both angels and demons, all around us.

SPIRITUAL BATTLE IN REAL TIME

There is much more to this universe than meets the eye. I learned this years ago during an evangelistic crusade in Pignon, Haiti. We had come at the invitation of Caleb Lucien, his brother Henoc, and his father, Sidoine, pastor of the Jerusalem Baptist Church. During the early days of the crusade, we had good services but there were no decisions. Then on Wednesday Henoc talked seriously with us about Satan's hold on the people.

That night I scrapped my prepared sermon and preached on "Who is greater—Satan or Jesus?" I began by talking about the big voodoo festival in nearby Cap-Haitien. Then I talked about who Satan is and where he came from. I explained Satan's character— a liar, a murderer, a deceiver, a slanderer, one who hates God and His Son, Jesus Christ, one who comes disguised as an angel of light. Finally I asked, "Who is greater—Satan or Jesus? If Satan, then serve him. If Jesus, then you must follow Him." To answer that question, I traced Satan's attempts to destroy Jesus—at His birth, in the temptation, through the demons, through Judas, in the garden, and finally at the cross. On Friday night, when Jesus was in the tomb, I said, the demons sang with joy and Satan danced in the fiery corridors of hell.

Then came Sunday and from the inside of the tomb a stirring, a sound, a movement. Jesus stood up, walked to the opening, walked through the stone, and stood outside the tomb. Jesus had come back from the dead! When I said that, the whole place erupted. Cheering, clapping, shouting, laughing, the Haitian believers joined in the great celebration. "And in hell, silence. The party was over. Satan had been defeated once and for all."

"The Witch Doctors Are Liars"

As we approached the invitation, I put the matter this way: "If you are following Satan, you are following a loser. He's been beaten. Jesus defeated him two thousand years ago, and he's still defeated today." Then I said the words that seemed to be the turning point of our whole trip: "The witch doctors are liars!" I shouted it out and the people roared with approval. I shouted it again: "The witch doctors are liars!" Then I said, "They are going to hell, and if you follow them, they will lead you straight to hell."

That was the galvanizing moment, the fulcrum, the turning point. Suddenly everything became clear. We had come to Haiti to do spiritual warfare against Satan and his followers. Then came the invitation, which in Haiti is a little different. They put a chair in front of the tabernacle facing the congregation. If you are going to accept Jesus, you're going to do it in full view of the audience, facing them so they can watch what happens. No halfway conversions in Haiti. Either go all the way or forget it. So we began to sing—the Creole version of "Hold the Fort." When we got to the part "Raise the standard high to heaven," everyone lifted hands in victorious praise. It was an awesome moment. After several minutes one person came forward. Eventually the tiny aisle was clogged with people coming forward and pastors meeting with them.

Who were these people? An assistant pastor's daughter. The daughter of a deaconess. All those who came forward had been part of the basketball camp our team was leading. And all of them said the same thing: They had been afraid to accept Christ because of fear of what Satan would do to them. Afterward Pastor Sidoine was ecstatic. The whole congregation stood and clapped and cheered and sang and rejoiced at the great victory God had won. Later Henoc would tell us that Wednesday night was the greatest service he had ever attended. Many of the team members felt the same way. I was reminded of the words of an old gospel song: "Heaven came down and glory filled my soul." This much I know: God was there that night. Nothing else can explain what happened.

Late that night—about 3 a.m.—we awakened to discover someone trying to climb on the roof of our building. One of our men actually saw his legs dangling over the roof. By the time we got outside he was gone. It was an eerie moment. Was it a thief? Possibly. Caleb speculated that it might be someone putting a voodoo curse on us by pouring some blood on our roof. (Such things routinely happen to him and his parents.)

Mad Men Muttering

Thursday was another story. Our final day in Pignon began with a two-hour couples conference on biblical sexuality. Then we had the final session of the Bible school and the final scrimmage of the basketball camp. As the afternoon wore on, Henoc came by with some striking news. He had been out and about in the community that day visiting the jail, the local judge, and a family from the church. Word filtered back, he said, that some people in Pignon were upset with me and the team. Why? Because of what I had said last night about the witch doctors being liars. That line, spoken off the cuff, had aroused the opposition. They didn't want anyone challenging their spiritual authority. The battle was now fully joined.

I sensed a different atmosphere the moment I arrived at the church that night. Gone was the joy and excitement of Wednesday night, replaced by a pensive awareness, a feeling of tension that you could almost reach out and touch. Something was about to happen.

Just before the service started, three men walked by dressed in red—voodoo practitioners on their way to a meeting with the devil. It was as if Satan was saying, "God may own the church, but I own the country." Meanwhile, as people continued to file in, motorcycles roared up and down the dirt road, revving their engines, trying to intimidate those who had come to worship. As the service began, the singing was not as joyful as the night before. The people seemed burdened, nervous, exhausted.

More than an hour passed before time came for me to preach my final message—"What will happen when Jesus returns?" I took as my text Matthew 24:37–39, which compares the days of Noah to the days when Jesus returns. I spoke of the unconcern and outright evil that marked Noah's day and compared it with modern-day Haiti. "There is no difference. The people of Noah's day weren't ready; the people of Pignon aren't ready." Unlike Wednesday when preaching seemed easy, every sentence was a struggle. I was aware of a strange muttering in the back of the sanctuary as I preached, but I didn't know what to make of it. Later I learned that twenty to thirty of the voodoo people had entered the back of the church, intending, if possible, to disrupt the service. They stayed in the back muttering curses and incantations as I preached.

Just before the invitation I reminded the people of Jesus' words: "Two shall be taken and one shall be left" (see Matt. 24:40). "What will happen to you when Jesus returns? Will you be taken or will you be left to face the judgment?" Then I walked up the middle aisle touching first one person and then another on the shoulder: "One will be taken, another left. One taken, another left."

"His Goat Has a Better Future Than He Does"

As the invitation began I was aware of great heaviness in the room. It seemed as if Jesus was in the front and Satan in the back, with the congregation hanging between heaven and hell. For nearly twenty minutes we sang with no response. Pastor Sidoine continually pleaded with the people to leave Satan and come to Jesus. At one point he told of a witch doctor who was traveling on a bus with his sacrificial goat when the bus was wrecked and the witch doctor and his goat were both killed. "That witch doctor went out into eternity without Jesus. His goat has a better future than he does."

Long after we would normally have ended the service, the invitation continued. It was now almost 10 p.m., and no one had come forward. Yet we were all aware of a vast struggle in the unseen realm of the spirit. Suddenly one girl came forward, then another—both in tears. The pastors met with them for a long time as we continued to sing. Finally Henoc came and told me the problem: "Those two girls have been demon-possessed in the past. They come from a voodoo family. They're afraid to accept Jesus because they fear Satan will attack them somehow. They keep begging us not to stop praying, because if we stop praying, they fear Satan will inhabit them again." This was far beyond anything I had ever experienced. I stepped off the platform, walked to find the other team members, told them the story, and asked them to pray. At that very moment others began to come forward. One by one they sat facing the audience, many with tears, confessing Jesus Christ as Lord.

The most dramatic moment came when a girl in her late teens stood up to come forward, and her friends grabbed her arm to pull her back down. There was a struggle, and then she broke free and came forward to accept Christ. Henoc prayed with her personally. She didn't want to pray herself, but he said, "You have to." She was scared to pray, scared of what Satan would do to her; but Henoc told her that if she wanted Jesus in her heart, she had to ask Him herself. She prayed and asked Jesus to be her Lord and Savior. In the end twelve people came forward, making a total of at least thirty people who trusted Christ during our trip. Most of them were young adults, most of them came from some voodoo background, and most of them were afraid of what Satan would do to them if they accepted Christ.

I have never seen anything like it. It was heaven or hell, God or Satan, streets of gold or the fires of hell. And nothing in between. At the end of the night I walked out into the darkness utterly exhausted, every ounce of strength drained from my body. I sat in the darkened road feeling not victorious, but as if I had just finished a fifteen-round boxing match.[4]

THE CHIEF WEAPONS
OF OUR SPIRITUAL WARFARE

I find this final point most encouraging: Since we can't see the angels and the demons, we don't need to worry about what they are doing. Our part is to walk humbly before the Lord, to seek His face in prayer, to grow in knowledge from the Word of God, and to persevere in faithfulness no matter how tough the times may be.

When I think about the Christians whose faith I admire, I immediately think of those who are going through hard times. I think of friends who worry that their daughter may have leukemia. I know others who struggle against cancer that has returned after years of remission. I received an e-mail from a young man whose parents are contemplating a divorce. He wrote me because I performed their wedding ceremony more than a quarter century ago. I received a note from a sailor who fights the battle against temptation and asked for my advice. Many others struggle with health issues or pray earnestly for God to move on their behalf.

I am struck by the words of the angel in Daniel 10:19: "Do not be afraid, O man highly esteemed," he said. "Peace! Be strong now; be strong." Twice he says "Be strong," as if he knows how tired Daniel is and how easy it would be to give up altogether.

This is God's Word to all of us today. Are you under attack from the Enemy? Never give up! Do you feel like quitting? Never give up! Are you fighting for your marriage? Never give up! Are you trying to be strong in the face of temptation? Never give up! Do you face a barrage of criticism for doing what you know is right? Never give up! Are you tired of the struggle? God's Word is clear. Never give up.

Man or woman of God, take courage. *Keep your eyes on Jesus.* Run to the Cross when you feel faint. Lean heavily on the Lord.

Are you tempted to quit? Pick up your armor and get back in the battle. When the day is done, you will be standing on the side of victory. Let nothing turn you aside. Fear not, and fight on.

Never give up. Never, never, never, never, *never* give up.

Stand your ground for Jesus Christ. And never give up.

FOUR

THE DEVIL'S
FOOTHOLD

"No man can think clearly when his fists are clenched."

—**GEORGE JEAN NATHAN**

THE DAY IS OVER AT LAST. You climb into bed ready to sleep, but sleep won't come. You toss and turn. You try sleeping on your side, your back, your front. You cover your head with the pillow, you turn on the fan, you open the window. You get up and take a shower. You go to the kitchen and make a sandwich. You sit down and watch TV, but you can't concentrate.

Nothing helps. You're dead tired and you had a rotten day. Your body cries out for rest and your eyes will hardly stay open. But your mind won't cooperate. What was it you said at supper? Ah, now it all comes back. The kids heard it too, didn't they? You said it in a blinding flash of anger. Now you wish you could take it back. Too late. Now it's nearly midnight. And you can't sleep. But you aren't the only one. Someone else is awake too—maybe crying, maybe silent, wondering when you will strike again. Take a good look at yourself. How many nights has it been lately? Maybe that's why you are so irritable and grouchy.

There is no easy way out . . . and you don't deserve one. No need to pray or wait for God's leading. You know what you have to do. Someone else is waiting for you to make the first move.

"Sweetheart, I was wrong and I know it. Please forgive me."

A MESSAGE FOR HOTHEADS

How difficult those words are to say. But every husband, every wife must say them sooner or later. And most of us will say them many times. Sometimes we speak of "losing" our temper as if we don't know where it is. The truth is, you never lose your temper; you simply turn it loose on someone else, usually someone close to you, often against those you love the most. Anger is a powerful emotion that can be used for good or for evil.

Anger isn't always wrong. We know, for instance, that anger is one of God's emotions. We know that God never sins, yet the Bible speaks of His anger in more than a hundred different passages. We also know that there are times when anger is justified and even righteous. Ephesians 4:26 says, "In your anger do not sin."

When we see people hurting other people, when we watch the wholesale slaughter of the unborn, when we see children being lured into drugs and prostitution, when we see families torn apart by sin, that ought to make us angry. If we sit idly by while the world goes to hell, if we don't get angry, if we don't weep, if we don't care, then something is wrong deep inside us. Romans 12:9 instructs us, "Hate what is evil; cling to what is good." If we do not do the former, we will not be able to do the latter. Our anger can motivate us toward a ministry that God has in place just for us. Our anger can show us where the wrong things have become priorities in our lives and families.

Before the Sun Goes Down

However, anger can quickly lead us in the wrong direction. Rather than bringing us to right the world's wrongs, it can lead us to putting our own desires ahead of our loved ones. The same verse that says, "In your anger do not sin," adds this phrase, "Do not let the sun go down while you are still angry" (Eph. 4:26b). That is, don't go to bed angry. Ephesians 4 looks at anger in our relationships. *Even if your anger is justified, don't go to sleep that way.* Deal with it, talk it out, pray it out, walk it out, but don't try to sleep it off. That won't work.

Recently I talked with a friend who mentioned another couple having serious marriage problems. He said, "I think for a long time they just neglected their relationship." You could say that about most couples who have problems. Little things build up . . . build up . . . and build up, like the lava in Mount Saint Helens and then, Boom! the top blows off.

There is a divine time limit on your anger. Solve your problems before you go to bed. Don't go to sleep angry. Why is that so important? *Because what you think about as you drift off to sleep becomes part of your subconscious.* What starts as anger overnight becomes a grudge by morning. The anger sinks in and slowly turns to resentment. Over time it hardens like concrete. Each little grudge becomes another brick in the wall that separates you from your mate. As long as you carry a grudge, you can't communicate with your spouse or your children. You talk but your mate hears only the anger inside. You try to listen but your resentment blocks the message from coming through clearly. Your negative emotions have clogged the pipeline. As a result, the sludge of a bad attitude clogs up the communication line, and nothing really gets through.

Commenting on this principle, my friend Brian Bill wrote the following note:

> Beth and I were challenged to make a vow before we were married to not ever let the sun go down on our anger. The pastor who married us read from Ephesians 4, and we then vowed

before God and the pastor to not ever go to bed angry. That was over ten years ago. I can say that this has been the best *single bit of advice we have ever received. We have never gone to bed angry yet—but we've sure had some late nights talking things out before we fall asleep.*

The very next verse in Ephesians offers this warning: "Do not give the devil a foothold" (4:27). All rock climbers understand that verse. In order to get up the side of the mountain, you've got to get a firm foothold. That's what Satan wants to do in your life—he wants to use your anger (even your legitimate anger) to get a foothold in your heart.

Daddy King

They called him "Daddy King." When Martin Luther King Sr. died in 1984, one black leader said, "If we started our own country, he would be our George Washington." In his eighty-four years he endured more than his share of suffering and hatred. During his childhood in Georgia, he witnessed lynchings. The first time he tried to register to vote in Atlanta, he found that the registrar's office was on the second floor of city hall—but the elevator was marked Whites Only, the stairwell was closed, and the elevator for blacks was out of order.

He is mostly remembered for the accomplishments of his son, the Reverend Martin Luther King Jr.—leader of the nonviolent civil rights movement, cut down by an assassin's bullet in 1968. In 1969, his second son drowned in a backyard swimming pool. The crowning blow came in 1974 during a church service. As his wife played "The Lord's Prayer," a young man rose in the congregation and began shooting. Mrs. King collapsed in a hail of gunfire while Daddy King watched in horror from the pulpit.

Near the end of his life, reflecting on the loss of his wife and oldest son, he spoke of the policy of nonviolence he had come to embrace. "There are two men I am supposed to hate. One is a white man, the other is black, and both are serving time for having committed murder. I don't hate either one. There is no time for that, and no reason either. Nothing that a man does takes him lower than when he allows himself to fall so low as to hate anyone."

But how can a man not hate when his wife and oldest son have been murdered? It seems natural and even proper to hate killers, doesn't it? The answer comes back, "There is no time for that." To hate is to live in the past, to dwell on deeds already done. Hatred is the most damaging emotion, for it gives the person you hate a double victory—once in the past, once in the present. No time to hate? Not if you have learned how to forgive. Forgiving does *not* mean whitewashing the past, but it does mean refusing to live there. Forgiveness breaks the awful chain of bitterness and the insidious desire for revenge. As costly as it is to forgive, unforgiveness costs far more.

THE COMMAND

In the same passage where Paul warned about giving the devil a foothold through unrighteous anger, he gave this solemn command: "Do not let any unwholesome talk come out of your mouths, but only what is helpful for building others up according to their needs, that it may benefit those who listen" (Eph. 4:29). Whenever I read that verse, my mind goes back to a speech class I took in college. The teacher was a young man in his first or second year of teaching. He was friendly and wise and very earnest. On the first day of class he said we were going to take a verse of Scripture as our theme for the semester. He picked Ephesians 4:29, which we repeated every time we met.

Back then everything we learned came from the King James Version, so that's how I remember it: "Let no corrupt communication proceed out of your mouth, but that which is good to the use of edifying, that it may minister grace unto the hearers." What the NIV translates as "unwholesome talk," the King James translates as "corrupt communication." The underlying Greek word means "rotten." It was used for decaying flesh, rotten fish, or rotten fruit.

The meaning is, "Don't let any putrid words come out of your mouth." We might say in street lingo, "No trash talk!"

What qualifies as rotten speech? Here are a few examples: Vulgarity, obscenity, indecent language. Racial or ethnic insults. Humor meant to put someone down. Angry outbursts, harsh words. Mean-spirited comments. Gossip, rumors, false accusations. Imputing bad motives. Public criticism of your spouse or children. Yelling and screaming. Threats and intimidating comments. Quick, cutting comments. Cheap shots. Talking too much or talking without listening. Exaggerating the faults of others. Excusing unkind words by saying, "I was only joking."

The Greek construction of Ephesians 4:29 is a bit unusual. The verse opens with a Greek word that means "all, each, every." The word meaning *no* occurs later in the verse. That gives a particular emphasis to his words:

Every critical comment that comes out of your mouth . . . not!

Every filthy word that comes out of your mouth . . . not!

Every harsh word that comes out of your mouth . . . not!

Every cheap shot that comes out of your mouth . . . not!

Every bit of gossip that comes out of your mouth . . . not!

SET ON FIRE BY HELL

Why is this so important? Proverbs 18:21 says, "The tongue has the power of life and death." Every time you open your mouth, either life or death comes out. The Bible speaks of the throat as an "open grave" (Rom. 3:13). When there is death on the inside, it will eventually show up in your words. According to Proverbs 12:18, "Reckless words pierce like a sword, but the tongue of the wise brings healing." And James 3:5–6 offers this penetrating warning:

Likewise the tongue is a small part of the body, but it makes great boasts. Consider what a great forest is set on fire by a small spark. The tongue also is a fire, a world of evil among the

70

parts of the body. It corrupts the whole person, sets the whole course of his life on fire, and is itself set on fire by hell.

Ephesians 4:29 offers a Christian alternative: First, we are to speak good words that build up instead of tearing down. Second, we are to speak words that minister grace to those who hear them. And we are to do it all the time and in every circumstance. We are to speak good words that bring grace according to the need of the moment. Here is the teaching of the verse put very simply: Every word . . . all good . . . all grace . . . all the time.

Sometimes we need a friend to remind us to watch what we say. Gordon MacDonald tells the story of a trip to Japan he took as a young man. One day, while walking the streets of Yokohama with an older pastor, he made a quick, sarcastic comment about a mutual friend. The older pastor stopped, looked him in the face, and said, "A man who truly loves God would not talk about a friend like that." Gordon MacDonald said it was as if a knife had been plunged between his ribs. The pain was so great that he didn't know how to respond. Reflecting on that experience twenty years later, he remarked that the memory of those searing words had helped him ten thousand times when he was tempted to make a critical comment about a family member, a friend, a colleague, or someone he knew casually.

We all have our excuses for what we say, don't we? We're tired or we're provoked or we weren't thinking or we didn't mean it or it's true so we said it. On and on we go, justifying our verbal diarrhea. We all have people in our lives who drive us nuts. Some people just know how to get under our skin. It might be a friend or a spouse or our children. It certainly could be an ex-husband or an ex-wife.

What is God saying to us? No more stinking speech!

The Consequence

Paul mentions the sad consequence of our unkind words in Ephesians 4:30: "And do not grieve the Holy Spirit of God, with whom you were sealed for the day of redemption." Did you know that you could grieve the Holy Spirit who lives within you? You can only grieve a close friend or a loved one. You can't grieve a stranger you meet on the street. You can irritate a stranger and you can offend a casual acquaintance, but you can only grieve someone very close to you. As usual, Paul's advice is both practical and profound. We tend to talk a lot about interpersonal problems, as if the greatest issue in life is how we relate to other people. But verse 30 reminds us that our primary relationship is always with God. And it is possible to grieve God's Holy Spirit. You can make the Spirit weep because of your thoughtless words.

Here's the reason: *The Holy Spirit not only lives in you. He also lives in the Christian brother or sister you just slandered with your lips.* Evil speech destroys Christian unity. D. L. Moody commented that he had never known God to bless a church where the Lord's people were divided. This is a word we need to hear today. This is God's Word to every church and all church leaders. We tolerate and sometimes even encourage thoughtless attitudes in the way we speak to each other and about each other. Every time I speak carelessly, I hurt at least four people:

(1) The person I speak carelessly about

(2) Myself

(3) The person to whom I speak

(4) The Holy Spirit

Every time I open my mouth, one of two things will happen:

(1) I build someone up, or

(2) I tear someone down.

This does not mean that we will never say anything hard or difficult for others to hear. The warning goes to motive or purpose and must be judged by the context. Proverbs 27:6 reminds us, "Faithful are the wounds of a friend" (KJV). Sometimes true friends "wound" each other in order to bring healing. Just as a doctor must sometimes cut us surgically in order to remove what is killing us, true friends sometimes say things that aren't easy to hear. But in those cases, true friends first remove the telephone pole from their own eye before they remove the speck of sawdust from someone else's eye.

The Cause

We grieve the Spirit first by rotten speech (Eph. 4:29) and second by rotten attitudes (v. 31). But these two things are not separate. Out of the abundance of the heart, the mouth speaks. Whatever is in the heart must eventually come out in the words we say. Whatever is down in the well will come up in the bucket sooner or later. "Let all bitterness and wrath and anger and clamor and slander be put away from you, along with all malice" (v. 31 NASB). These words describe a collection of wrong attitudes that corrode the soul from the inside out. First there is bitterness, a word that means "pointed" or "sharp," referring to the pain we feel when we think we've been mistreated. It speaks to a deep emotional reaction that keeps us from thinking clearly. If we dwell in bitterness long enough, it produces a wounded spirit and a hard heart.

The second word is wrath, a word that originally meant "to snort." It has the idea of the nostrils being flared in anger. This is hot-tempered anger that explodes under the slightest provocation. We use the same image when we speak of someone being all steamed up, with smoke coming out of his ears.

Anger, the third word, speaks of a settled condition of the heart. Did you ever know a person who was angry all the time? One Sunday when I asked that question in my sermon, two young girls nodded their heads vigorously. Some people get up angry, shower angry, eat breakfast angry, go to work angry, come home angry, watch TV angry, and go to bed angry. And when they are happy, that makes them angry. Nothing pleases a person like that. Anger leads to jealousy, harsh words, and it can even lead to murder.

Angry people usually express themselves in brawling or clamor, the fourth word, which means "raising your voice." It includes all forms of physical and verbal intimidation. It has the idea of shouting back and forth during a quarrel. How many arguments could be avoided if we didn't raise our voices? "A gentle answer turns away wrath, but a harsh word stirs up anger" (Prov. 15:1).

Paul uses a very strong word for slander, the fifth word, to describe this form of evil speaking. It means "to make false accusations about someone or to offer vague insinuations that make another person look worse than he really is." We can slander with our words, with a lifted eyebrow, with an unfinished sentence, with a rhetorical question left dangling in the air, or by quoting others but taking their words and twisting them into something sinister. We can slander through insults, ridicule, cruel jokes, taunts, unkind nicknames, rumors, mocking, belittling, or passing unfair and hasty judgment. In legal terms this is called "defamation of character."

Words give us control over others. *Every word we say affects our relationships for good or for ill.* Once a slanderous word escapes our lips, our relationship is changed forever. This was one of the sins of those who crucified Jesus. They mocked Him and lied about Him and falsely accused Him. As a result of their slander, the Son of God was crucified. When you slander someone, you join with those who crucified our Lord.

Malice, the final word, describes an underlying attitude of ill will. It's a general dislike of others. Malice can be described as congealed hatred. A malicious person can't get along with anyone.

What starts in the heart ends up on the lips. We think, we feel, and then we speak. What starts as a grievance becomes an outburst of wrath that hardens into anger that expresses itself in clamor and ultimately as slander. Malice marks such a person through and through. And it all starts with personal hurt that becomes bitterness. Stop it at the first and you won't have to stop it at the last. That's why Proverbs 4:23 reminds us to "guard your heart, for it is the wellspring of life."

Note that Paul says to get rid of *all* these wrong attitudes:

No root of bitterness

No symptoms of wrath

No trace of anger

No echo of clamor

No slime of slander

No dregs of malice

As long as we harbor these things, the Holy Spirit weeps inside us.

From God to Us to Others

Those things must go . . . and be replaced with something much better. "Be kind and compassionate to one another, forgiving each other, just as in Christ God forgave you" (Eph. 4:32).

Kindness speaks of gentleness in the face of provocation. It reaches out to the unworthy and withholds punishment even when it is deserved. Kindness is daring and dangerous because some people mistake it for weakness. It is "the oil that lubricates the machinery of life." Compassion says, "I will care for you, and I will not shut you out."

Forgiveness starts with God, comes down to us, and then goes out to other people. This is what Ephesians 4:32 plainly says. We are to forgive as God has forgiven us. In his massive commentary on Ephesians, Harold Hoehner points out that the word translated *forgive* in the NIV is actually a Greek word meaning "be gracious." It includes forgiveness but is actually a much broader concept. We are to extend grace to others as God has extended grace to us. We, the undeserving who have been showered with God's grace in Christ, are to give to other undeserving sinners (who have sinned against us) the same outpouring of grace. From God to us to others. Grace to us, grace to others. This is God's plan.[1]

We do for others what God has done for us. We have been forgiven; we know what it is like. We are not left to wonder what it means to forgive those who have hurt us. You cannot understand

God's love unless you go to the cross. You cannot understand the cross unless you see in it God's love.

His death became a sacrifice that was a sweet aroma to the Father (Eph. 5:1–2). Man's murder became God's sacrifice. A heinous crime paid an impossible debt. Through the death of an innocent man, we, the guilty, go free. If we had been there, the stench of death would have overwhelmed us, but the cross smelled good to the Father.

> *See, from his hands, his feet, his head*
> *Sorrow and love flow mingled down!*
> *Did e'er such love and sorrow meet,*
> *Or thorns compose so rich a crown?*

Pastor Demitri

God asks us to do what He has already done for us. We are not to forgive in order to be forgiven. We forgive *because* we have been forgiven. Several years ago I spoke at a Bible conference in northern Wisconsin on the topic of forgiveness. During each session, a tall woman sat directly in front of me. After one message she introduced herself and told me a bit of her story, which included her own struggles with forgiveness. A few days later I received the following letter:

> *Dear Pastor Pritchard,*
>
> *I left camp with a full heart yesterday. Thank you for your ministry among us. I am the tall woman who sat pretty much front and center to you. Your last message was deeply challenging to me to go beyond just forgiving to the point of neutrality. Since Christ commanded that we be proactive in this matter, it can only be done by His power. Humanly speaking I am bankrupt. Just where He wants me.*

Then she added a little smiley face in the text and continued, "I carried the enclosed article around in my Bible for several years. I can't tell you how many times I have read and reread it. I want you to have a copy for your illustration file." She enclosed a photocopy of an article by Richard Wurmbrand published in the December 1998 issue of *Voice of the Martyrs*. Pastor Wurmbrand spent fourteen years in a communist jail in Romania. This is the story of a man named Demitri who was in prison with him.

Demitri was beaten with a hammer, paralyzing him, making him a quadriplegic. The other prisoners cared for him as best they could without access to running water or good facilities—but the other prisoners were on work duties all day long. Demitri lay in his own filth day by day, in pain and alone until the evening. In December 1989, Romania's revolution freed Demitri to the care of his family. Let's pick up the story from there.

> *One day someone knocked at his door. It was the Communist who had crippled him. He said, "Sir, don't believe that I have come to ask forgiveness from you. For what I have done, there is no forgiveness, not on earth or in heaven. You are not the only one I have tortured like this. You cannot forgive me; nobody can forgive me. Not even God. My crime is much too great. I have come only to tell you that I am sorry about what I have done. From you I go to hang myself. That is all." He turned to leave.*
>
> *The paralyzed brother Demitri said to him, "Sir in all these years I have not been so sorry as I am now, that I cannot move my arms. I would like to stretch them out to you and embrace you. For years I have prayed for you every day. I love you with all my heart. You are forgiven."*[2]

Demitri forgave because he knew Jesus forgave him. If you want to know what love is like, go to Golgotha and fix your eyes on the man hanging from the center cross. *Study what He did, and you will know true love.* What sort of man is this who dies on a Roman cross—willingly?

He was a good man, a teacher of God's law, a man who helped

those in need and got angry only when He saw injustice in the world. He never had a great education. He never held public office. He never wrote a book. He never traveled more than two hundred miles from the place where He was born. His own family thought He was a bit strange. They never really understood why He did what He did or said what He said.

When He started His ministry, the powers that be at first found Him a nuisance and later a threat. They sent their best people to try to trip Him up on technicalities, but it never worked. He was too smart to be fooled by slick questions. But every time He made them look foolish, it just made them angrier. Eventually, they decided that He must be killed. But because He was popular with the common people, they couldn't arrest Him carelessly. They had to find a reason, a plausible excuse, something that would give them a cover for their dirty deeds.

The day came when He traveled to the capital city for a public celebration. Thousands of people were there that week. Multitudes lined the narrow streets as He rode on a donkey into the city. "God save us!" they cried. "God save us!" For almost a week He taught publicly, answering questions, debating His opponents, preparing His followers for what was to come.

Finally, the leaders decided to make their move. They had found a man among His followers—His treasurer, no less—who was willing to sell Him out in exchange for a handful of money. The deal was struck, the time set, the plan made. It all went like clockwork, and the good man was arrested.

Dirty Justice

Five times He was tried, before four different judges. The charges weren't really clear, but it was something about blasphemy and then something about treason. At one hearing, the witnesses openly contradicted one another. But it didn't matter. So great was their hatred, so deep their anger, so fierce their rage that truth didn't count. "This man must die!" they said. Let justice be damned!

He was cruelly beaten. Ridiculed. Spat upon. Mocked. Humiliated.

Tortured until His flesh hung in ribbons. Beaten until He was barely conscious. Stripped naked. Condemned to die. Forced to carry the instrument of His own death. Outside the city walls, near a limestone quarry with the strange face of a skull outlined on the side of a cliff, the good man was put to death. The Bible says that the passersby stopped when they saw Him; then they joined the jeering crowd gone mad with bloodlust. It was an awful scene, proof that the human mind is capable of the very worst atrocities.

You were there. So was I. So was everyone who ever walked on this sin-cursed planet. All of us were there that day. Not to help, but to hurt. To join the rabble crying, "Crucify Him! Crucify Him!" We were all there watching the good man die, doing nothing to save Him, nothing to ease His pain. We were there. And He saw us. He saw you. And He saw me. He knew you by name. And He knew me too. All of us joined in that terrible moment. All of us cheered when the nails drove through the flesh. All of us laughed when He screamed in agony.

The whole human race was there, laughing as the Son of God died.

Father, Forgive Them!

He didn't say much that day, only seven or eight sentences. But, oh, what words they were. What power! What truth He spoke!

Do you remember the first words He said from the cross? How could you ever forget them? He looked down, His chest heaving, the sun beating on His fevered, bleeding brow, His face a mass of blood and tears, His hands and feet dripping blood from the nail holes. He saw the laughter, heard the jeers, and knew that they were laughing at Him.

He had done nothing wrong. Nothing to deserve this.

He closed his eyes, as if in prayer. Then he looked again at the howling, wild mob. "Father, forgive them, for they do not know what they are doing" (Luke 23:34).

Forgive them? But they were guilty of the greatest crime in all history.

Forgive them? But He was innocent . . . and they knew it.

Forgive them? But they had twisted the truth, made up lies, slandered His name, bribed His treasurer, rigged the trial, and guaranteed His death. It was murder, pure and simple. They meant to kill Him . . . and they did.

Forgive them? How could it be?

He was a good man, the best man the world has ever seen. He came to show us how to live, and He came to show us how to die. He came to save us while we were yet sinners. He even came to save those who put Him to death. "Father, forgive them." I'm so glad Jesus said that, because it shows us that forgiveness is always possible. If He could forgive, then anything is possible. If the Son of God could rise above anger and hatred, if He could find a way to forgive His enemies, then so can we—with His strength, not our own.

FOUR STEPS TO FREEDOM

How do you handle your anger so that it doesn't destroy you? Here are four simple suggestions.

1. Have the Courage to Face Your Anger.

It all begins here. Until you can admit to the "other face" that no one ever sees, you will never be able to get past it. So many of us have a public face that looks good and a private face that we keep behind locked gates and stone walls, a face of anger and hatred. Let me say that I have learned from hard personal experience the truth of what I am talking about. I know what it is to lose my temper in a critical moment and say things I regret later. For me, the healing didn't begin until I could say, "I got angry and lost my temper. The rest doesn't matter. I have to own up to my own problems."

2. Discuss Your Struggles with a Friend.

Men especially seem to struggle in this area. We harbor deep feelings and don't know what to do with them. What's worse, we're afraid to tell anyone because we think that sharing our struggles is a sign of weakness. How wrong we are. The weak cover up; only the strong have the courage to admit they need help.

3. Do a Relationship Inventory Based on Ephesians 4:30–32.

These words are incredibly specific. Check your life for any signs of bitterness, anger, rage, slander, brawling, and malice. If you find even a trace of those things, get rid of them. They are like a virus in your spiritual bloodstream.

Anger kills. Bitterness kills. Slander kills. Rage kills. Resentment kills. They don't just kill other people. They kill you too!

4. Yield Control of Your Life to the Holy Spirit.

You can have the Holy Spirit in control, or your anger can take control. There is no third option and no middle ground. Jesus has shown us the way. You don't have to live in anger and bitterness over the way people treat you, or the way someone treated you in the past. God's Spirit can set you free from the chains that bind you to the past. You've got to give up your anger; let go of your bitterness; say farewell to your hurtful memories. Then and only then will the Holy Spirit be free to take control of your life.

But you say, "I can't do that. You don't know what they did to me." What if God treated you as you treat others? You'd be in hell already. What if God were as unkind and unmerciful as you are? What if He kept a record of your sins and refused to forgive them? You'd never get within a million miles of heaven.

"I'm going to trash him like he trashed me." What if God said that about you?

"I don't know how much I can take." How much did Jesus take for you?

Do you want to know what troubles me most about this text with its warning against rotten speech and rotten attitudes that grieve the Spirit? I see far too much of myself in it. It is so easy for me to be unkind and ungracious. Between services one Sunday, when I was preaching on this topic, I had a few moments to chat with a friend. He made some quip about a third person who was not present, and I made a quip back—a comment I should not have made. As my friend walked away, I felt immediately pricked in my conscience. Even after preaching this sermon, I found it all too easy to violate the very thing I was trying to say to others. So I confess my own weakness and ask the Lord to baptize my mouth, sanctify my lips, and transform my heart.

Maybe you need the same thing. Perhaps you need to have a heart-to-heart talk with the Lord and then with others close to you. A woman came up to me in tears and said, "I've been so hard on my children. I'm going to go home, get them all together, and ask for their forgiveness." That's hard to do, but it's also the path of true spiritual liberation.

Whatever God tells you to do, do it. Stop making the Holy Spirit weep because of your unkind words and your inner ugliness. Cry out to God for His help. Ask the Lord to open your eyes and see the uncleanness within. Pray for a fresh vision of Jesus dying for you.

Stop giving the devil a foothold in your life.

Stop making the Holy Spirit weep.

FIVE

LESSONS FROM CHAIRMAN MAO

"You can be sure of succeeding in your attacks if you only attack places that are undefended."

—SUN TZU, THE ART OF WAR

MY WIFE AND I TRAVELED TO BEIJING to visit one of our sons who was teaching English in China for a year. We set aside one day to do some sightseeing we hadn't been able to do on our first trip a year earlier. After a quick visit to the Temple of Heaven, we took a cab to Tiananmen Square, a large plaza in central Beijing adjacent to the Forbidden City and the site of massive pro-democracy rallies in 1989. On one side of the vast square is a museum showcasing China's thousands of years of civilization. On the other side you find the building housing the Chinese parliament. On the end opposite the Forbidden City are several ancient gates from the days when emperors ruled the Middle Kingdom.

As you wander around the square, you see soldiers here and there, quite a few police, and (if the weather is good) strolling couples and families taking pictures. You continually run into vendors hawking everything from "genuine Rolexes" for twenty dollars (although you can bargain them down to less than two dollars) to kites, postcards, buttons, medallions, T-shirts, and camera batteries. The middle of the square is dominated by a statue honoring the "heroes of the Chinese revolution," meaning the supporters of Mao Tse-tung and the Communist Party. To the right as you face the statue, Chairman Mao lies in state in an enormous mausoleum, more than thirty years after his death in 1976.

NO PICTURES ALLOWED

This is why we had come to Tiananmen Square on a cold morning in January. Beijing in January is just as cold as Chicago in January, only without the snow. We came because I wanted to view the preserved remains of Chairman Mao. Upon approaching the entrance, we encountered the kind of line you find at an airport security checkpoint. The Chinese have one rule above all others regarding Chairman Mao's body. No pictures. They are ironclad about it and apparently make no exceptions. If you have a camera, you must surrender it before you get in line. A guard came up to me, patted down my thick overcoat, and pointed me forward.

We stood in line (outside) for a few minutes with approximately 100 to 150 others, mostly Chinese with a few foreigners in the mix. I noticed quite a few families with young children. When the word was given, the soldiers allowed our group to go forward. Signs and a voice from a loudspeaker repeatedly warned us not to take pictures.

After being herded around a corner, we stopped near a kiosk where an announcement was made (in Chinese) that we could buy flowers to place at the base of Chairman Mao's statue inside the mausoleum. A friend had told us earlier that the flowers are a good moneymaker because the government sells the flowers, people put them at the base of the statue, and after everyone is through, workers pick up the flowers, take them outside to the kiosk, and sell them again. Twenty or thirty people in our group brought flowers.

Inside the building, everywhere were guards watching us and moving us along. In the first room, a rotunda of sorts, we passed an enormous statue of Chairman Mao. He was seated on a chair with his legs crossed. It vaguely reminded me of the Lincoln Memorial with its massive statue of President Lincoln filling the building. The statue of Chairman Mao wasn't as big, but the effect was the same. As we passed the statue, people with flowers came forward and bowed before it. Some knelt in tribute, placing their flowers at the feet of the chairman. It was an eerie, surreal scene.

Very quickly the line moved to the next room where we would see the mortal remains of Mao Tse-tung. The line split in two as we filed past the dimly lit casket. A grim-faced woman moved us along very quickly. No one had time to stop and look. The casket rests on a platform behind a thick glass barrier that runs from ceiling to floor. As we passed by, I caught a glimpse of Mao's face, frozen in death, pallid, grayish-brown, and waxen in appearance. Even as I typed these words, a shudder came over me as I thought about my brief encounter with one of the most influential dictators of modern times.

THE LITTLE RED BOOK

As soon as we entered the next room, the guards disappeared. This was the gift shop where we could buy all sorts of Mao-related souvenirs. As we descended the stone steps at the rear of the mausoleum, we were surrounded by enterprising Chinese vendors. One friendly chap wanted to sell us Mao's famous "Little Red Book." We dickered with him for a minute or two, then went on our way. He followed us, lowering his price as we walked. Finally I purchased a copy of *The Quotations from Chairman Mao Tse-tung* for 15 yuan (a little less than $2). The book is pocket-sized, with a red plastic cover bearing the face of Mao embossed on the plastic, surrounded by little yellow rays of sun. The book contains

590 pages, the left-hand pages in Chinese, the right-hand pages giving the English translation.[1]

I had more than a passing interest in the book because of its historical importance. There was a time in China when everyone had his own copy of the "Little Red Book" and studied it religiously. That was especially true during the cultural revolution of the 1960s and early '70s. I wanted my own copy for another reason. According to a 2001 survey, Chairman Mao's "Little Red Book" is the second-best-selling book of all time. The Bible is the best-selling book in history, with at least six billion copies in print. But the "Little Red Book" has sold more than nine hundred million copies. For that alone, it deserves to be read and studied.

70 Million

A recent biography called *Mao: The Unknown Story* by Jung Chang and Jon Halliday begins with this sentence: "Mao Tse-tung, who for decades held absolute power over the lives of one-quarter of the world's population, was responsible for well over 70 million deaths in peacetime, more than any other twentieth-century leader."[2]

Mao was one of the greatest killers of all time. As I perused the "Little Red Book," I ran across one of his more famous sayings, where he puts it very plainly: "Every Communist must grasp the truth, 'Political power grows out of the barrel of a gun'" (p. 121).

He speaks forcefully of the brutality necessary for a revolution to succeed:

> *A revolution is not a dinner party, or writing an essay, or painting a picture, or doing embroidery; it cannot be so refined, so leisurely and gentle, so temperate, kind, courteous, restrained and magnanimous. A revolution is an insurrection, an act of violence by which one class overthrows another.* (p. 23)

Then he adds this word to the fearful: "If you are afraid of war day in day out, what will you do if war eventually comes?" (p. 131).

How to Win Against a Superior Force

He speaks at one point of the importance of not going into battle unless you have overwhelming numeric superiority. In the beginning, the Communists were a minority on the battlefield. Their only hope was to pick spots where they could win one battle at a time.

A few pages later he said, "Without preparedness superiority is not real superiority and there can be no initiative either. Having grasped this point, a force that is inferior but prepared can often defeat a superior enemy by surprise attack" (p. 191).

This final quote deserves mention because it is the ultimate statement of asymmetric warfare. Preparation matters more than anything else in warfare, especially in a war that drags on and on. Today's terrorists understand this principle better than we do. The terrorists cannot win a head-on confrontation with the United States or with any other major power. But they can fly planes into buildings, blow up trains, incite people to riot over cartoons in a Danish newspaper, and kill soldiers and civilians with roadside bombs.

When Mao wrote these words, he led an army that fought against both the Nationalist Army and the Japanese Army. It would not have seemed likely that one day he would become the icon and demigod of all of China. It was by no means certain in 1938 that either the Japanese or the Nationalists would ever be defeated. Many things had to happen in order for Mao's army to win. But he understood the fundamental axiom of asymmetric warfare: *Find out where your enemy is unprepared, and hit him hard when he least expects it.*

ONE FRIDAY IN JERUSALEM

It happened one Friday morning in Jerusalem. The rooster crowed, and Peter never forgot it. The story itself was repeated over and over again by the first generation of Christians. They never forgot it, and they never tired of telling it. Wherever the story of

Jesus' arrest is told, the story of Peter and the rooster is sure to be told as well. Few Bible stories speak to us as this one does.

It is late on Thursday night in Jerusalem. Jesus has just been arrested and taken away to the house of the high priest. Most of the disciples are nowhere to be found. They are gone, scattered, drifted off into the darkness, too shocked and too angered by the actions of Judas to do anything else. When the crowd of soldiers led Jesus away, Peter decided to follow them. He had promised never to desert Jesus, and he wasn't going to start now. In the confusion it was easy to tag along behind the crowd. No one seemed to notice him. Certainly no one recognized him as one of Jesus' top men.

He followed the crowd to the house of the high priest. The house opened onto a courtyard that could only be entered through a gate near the alley. By the time Peter got there, the soldiers had taken Jesus inside to meet the high priest. The crowd had partly dispersed, it being late and the major excitement over for the time being. Some had gone home, and others were warming themselves by a fire in the courtyard. It was early April and the temperature had probably dropped into the upper forties.

It was hard to tell exactly how many people were there. There were soldiers milling about and servant girls running errands. Plus there were hangers-on and passersby (exactly the category Peter himself fit into) who were waiting to see what would happen to this fellow Jesus.

In order to understand what happens next, it helps to remember that it is now sometime after midnight. In the darkness Peter comes to the gate and waits to be admitted. No one there knows who he is (he thinks), so it should be perfectly safe for him to go in. True, he is now in enemy territory; but it's the middle of the night, and there's no reason for them to suspect him. Armed with that thought, he brushes past the servant girl on his way to stand by the fire in the courtyard.

Just as he was getting to the fire, the servant girl spoke up and said, "You were with that Nazarene, Jesus from Galilee." The words hit Peter like an electric shock. Somehow she recognized him.

How did she know him? It really didn't matter. And it didn't matter that she didn't know his name. What mattered was that somehow she had connected him with Jesus. Peter had to think fast.

Instinctively, he muttered out the oldest dodge in the world, "I don't know what you are talking about." That's right. Just play dumb. It worked. Or at least Peter thought it worked. But as he stood around the fire talking to the soldiers, he noticed two or three people looking at him closely. Too closely. Too carefully. One or two were nodding in his direction and whispering.

Minutes passed and Peter turned to walk out of the courtyard. Things were getting a little dicey. As he did, a second servant girl (a friend of the first) suddenly spoke up: "This fellow is one of them."

Peter tried to act calm, but he felt his heart pounding in his chest. *Quick now, you've got to say something. Think. Think. Don't just stand there.* So he said, "I don't know the man." But when he said it, his face was flushed and he could tell the girl didn't believe him.

Trapped!

Peter knew he was in real trouble. Talk about being in the wrong place at the wrong time. He was in the enemy camp warming himself at the enemy's fire. If he tried to leave now, that would arouse even more suspicion. But if he stayed, they might find him out. More time passed, with more looks and whispers directed at him.

After about an hour, it appeared that Jesus' interview with the high priest was about over. The guards were going to and from the house, and the tempo in the courtyard picked up. Peter breathed a sigh of relief. Maybe he would get out of this after all. Just at that moment a man spoke up from the other side of the fire. He sounded more sure of himself and definitely more hostile than the servant girls. "Didn't I see you with Him in the olive grove?" Peter looked up at him and tried to play dumb. This time it didn't work. Evidently this fellow had gone with the crowd to arrest Jesus.

Worse, he was a relative of Malchus, the man whose ear Peter had impulsively cut off.

Peter was trapped and he knew it. This fellow had *seen* him with Jesus. Plus, he was plenty ticked off about what Peter had done. When a man is backed into a corner, he will do almost anything to save himself. In this case, Peter began to curse and swear. "I don't know Him. Why don't you leave me alone? May God strike me dead if I have ever heard of this man Jesus." The words just came tumbling out, old words born of fear and exhaustion. Words Peter hadn't used since his days as a fisherman.

At the very instant the words flew from his mouth, a rooster began to crow.

The Devil's Hounds Run in Packs

What possessed Peter to deny knowing Jesus? The answer is not difficult to find. Peter was scared and he was tired. That doesn't excuse his conduct, but it does make it understandable. After all that had happened, Peter finally ran out of strength. Consider the matter from his point of view. Jesus' case appeared to be hopeless. They had Him at last, and they would not let Him go until He was dead. That much was clear. What point would there be in sticking his neck out?

Besides that, Peter was tired and lonely and cold and a little bit disoriented. Plus—and this is a big factor—he never expected to be questioned by a servant girl. Her question caught him totally off guard, and he blurted out an answer almost without thinking. But once he denied knowing Jesus, there was no turning back. He had to play out the string. That's part of the irony of this story. Peter denied Christ to a servant girl. Not to the high priest. Not to a soldier. Not to anyone important. He denied Christ to a menial maid. But one sin leads to another. Peter was like a confused sheep surrounded by a pack of wolves. His lack of courage when questioned by the servant girl made him more susceptible to the other questions that were soon to come. His confidence eroded, he became easy prey. Soon he had denied his Lord three times.

I think Peter was ready to die for Christ that night. A few hours earlier he was whacking off somebody's ear. Peter was no coward. And he knew the risk involved in going to the courtyard of the high priest. I think (though I cannot prove this) that if Peter had been brought before the high priest he would have said, "Yes, I am a follower of Jesus." With satisfaction, he would have followed his Master to the cross. That's the kind of man he was. What happened? *He was totally unprepared to be questioned by a servant girl.* She caught him off guard, and he lied about knowing Jesus. But one lie leads to another. As Alexander MacLaren put it, "One sin makes many. The Devil's hounds run in packs."

Peter's Seven Great Mistakes

What happened to Peter was no fluke. He set himself up by a long string of bad decisions. Here are the seven great mistakes he made that night:

1. **He talked when he should have been listening.** At the Last Supper, when Jesus said that all His disciples would desert Him, Peter impulsively blurted out, "Even if everyone else deserts you, I will never desert you." Within six hours Peter would come to regret those brave words.

2. **He didn't appreciate his own weakness.**

3. **He ignored Jesus' warning.**

4. **He followed afar off.** He followed Jesus, but at a distance, when he should have been at His elbow. In this case, following Jesus afar off only got him in more trouble.

5. **He warmed himself at the wrong fire.** Peter had no business warming himself in the company of the enemies of the Lord. By consorting with those who had arrested Jesus, Peter was placing himself in a position where he would almost certainly be exposed. Peter warmed himself by the wrong fire until things got too hot for him.

6. He was unprepared when the attack came.

7. He compounded his sin by first deceiving, then denying, and finally swearing. But this was inevitable. Peter set himself up for a fall, and when it came, it was a big one. "O what a tangled web we weave, when first we practice to deceive." It is interesting to note that Peter fooled only himself. The others never really believed him. They sensed he was lying. Something in his face and the tone of his voice gave him away.

And so it was that Peter—the "rock"—crumbled in the critical moment. He had denied his Lord not once, but three times. It was a failure he would remember for the rest of his days. As we think of it, let us take to heart the words of 1 Corinthians 10:12, "So, if you think you are standing firm, be careful that you don't fall!"

ATTACKING OUR
STRONG POINTS

Satan often attacks us at the point of our strength, not the point of our weakness. A few hours earlier Peter boldly declared, "Even if everyone else deserts you, I will never desert you." If you had asked Peter at that moment to name his strong points, no doubt he would have listed boldness and courage right at the top. He would have said, "Sometimes I put my foot in my mouth, but at least I'm not afraid to speak up. Jesus knows that I'll always be there when He needs me." But when Satan attacked, it came so suddenly, so swiftly, so unexpectedly that the bold apostle turned to butter. By himself Peter is helpless. In the moment of crisis, Peter fails in the very point where he pledged to be eternally faithful.

Should this surprise us? After all, why should Satan attack only in the point of your self-perceived weakness? If you know you have a weakness, that's the very area you will guard most carefully. If you know you have a problem with anger or with laziness or with lust or with gluttony, will you not be on your guard lest you fall?

But it is not so with your strengths. You take those areas for granted. You say, "That's not a problem for me. I have other problems, but that area is not really a temptation at all."

Watch out! Put up the red flag! There is danger ahead. When a person takes *any* area of life for granted, that's the one area Satan is most likely to attack. Why? Because that's the one area where you aren't watching for his attack.

It happened to Peter. It will happen to you and to me sooner or later.

Chairman Mao understood this point perfectly. Let me repeat that final quote one more time: "Without preparedness superiority is not real superiority and there can be no initiative either. Having grasped this point, a force that is inferior but prepared can often defeat a superior enemy by surprise attack."

That perfectly describes what happened to Peter. He meant well, but he wasn't prepared for what was about to hit him. He wasn't a coward, but he overestimated his own strength, and in a weak moment he was brought down by a teenage girl. Two thousand years later, we still remember that under pressure Peter caved in and denied the Lord. It's not surprising that many years later, Peter wrote these words: "Stay alert! Watch out for your great enemy, the devil. He prowls around like a roaring lion, looking for someone to devour" (1 Peter 5:8 NLT). Lions are awesome not only for their roar and their fearsome appearance. They are to be feared because they lie in wait, sometimes for hours, until an unsuspecting victim comes too close. By then it's too late. There is no escape. For Peter, the "roaring lion" came in the form of a servant girl who asked him a question he wasn't prepared to answer.

It was a classic case of asymmetric warfare, and it utterly defeated Peter.

There are many lessons here if we care to take them:

- The devil doesn't fight fair.

- He attacks when we least expect it.

- He attacks our strengths because we take them for granted.

- He attacks repeatedly from different angles.

- Any ground left unguarded becomes open territory for the devil.

Pay attention. Keep your eyes open. Don't brag. Stay close to Christ, and lean on your Christian friends. Put on the armor of God, and take up the sword of the Spirit. Pray like crazy.

The battle has been joined, the enemy doesn't fight fair, and every believer is on the front lines. Be prepared, lest you too should become a casualty in the battle. It's not always the big things that bring us down. Sometimes the small things do it, because we weren't prepared when the Enemy made his move.

SIX

A PRAYER FROM THE BATTLEFIELD

"Wars are not won by evacuations!"

—WINSTON CHURCHILL

ON THE DAY IN MARCH 2003 when the war in Iraq broke out, a Chicago TV station sent a news team to cover our special prayer meeting. Hoping to get some good sound bites, they interviewed several people from the congregation. When the reporter asked why we were having a prayer meeting at the very moment when the bombs were about to start falling, one woman gave a simple answer, "We believe our most powerful weapon is prayer." There is a world of truth in her words. The psalmist declared, "Some trust in chariots and some in horses, but we trust in the name of the LORD our God" (Psalm 20:7). In the last few years we have seen the marvels of modern technology: laser-guided bombs, missiles that can hit a tank under a bridge and leave the bridge standing, bombs guided by satellites, goggles that enable you to see at night, and planes that cannot be seen by radar. Fifteen years ago this was the stuff of science fiction. Now we sit at home and watch the war unfold in real time on television.

As amazing as those things are, they only touch the physical realm. We have a weapon far greater than anything we have seen in the war, a supernatural weapon—prayer. I hope in this chapter to encourage you to pray when you are in trouble.

GOD DELIVERS THROUGH PRAYER

During prayer meeting, a man said, "Lord, it's easy to get into trouble, but it's hard to get out of trouble." Psalm 50:15 offers this wonderful promise: "Call upon me in the day of trouble; I will deliver you, and you will honor me." When we are in trouble, God wants us to cry out to Him. "God is our refuge and strength, an ever-present help in trouble" (Ps. 46:1).

Our God delights to rescue His children when we are in desperate straits. "The righteous cry out, and the LORD hears them; he delivers them from all their troubles" (Ps. 34:17). God invites us to turn to Him when everything in the world has turned against us. When in trouble, pray! That may seem obvious, but sometimes we forget to pray. And sometimes we don't know how to pray. Second Thessalonians 3:1–5 gives us five requests that are always appropriate when trouble comes our way. Here are five ways to pray when our backs are against the wall.

The First Request: Effective Proclamation

"Pray for us that the message of the Lord may spread rapidly and be honored, just as it was with you" (2 Thess. 3:1). The first thing Paul asks is that people would pray for the proclamation of the gospel. In Greek the request is literally "that the Lord's message might run." Those of you who like to jog will appreciate this word picture. May the message of the gospel go quickly from city to city, from house to house, from one heart to another. His desire is for the gospel to have free course as it hurries into the hearts of hurting people.

He also wants this message to be *honored*, which means "to be magnified" or "to be rendered glorious." "Lord, let Your Word be received with the honor that it deserves." I encourage you to pray by name for the streets in your community. When I lived in Oak Park, Illinois, I prayed like this: "Lord, let Your Word run through Oak Park. Let it run through the high school. Let it run down Lake Street. Let it run through River Forest and Elmwood Park and Forest Park and Cicero and Berwyn and Riverside and into Chicago and in Hazel Crest and Harvey and Elmhurst and Oak Brook. O Lord, turn Your Word loose, and let it run from Oak Park to the ends of the earth!"

Paul makes a similar request in Colossians 4:3b, "That God may open a door for our message." In Greek this is literally "a door for the Word." The concept of "open doors" in the New Testament almost always has to do with new opportunities for spreading the gospel. It could include a brother or a sister, your parents or your children, or some other relative. It might be an open door to preach Christ in a new town or a new country. The idea is that Christ Himself opens and shuts the doors of opportunity (Rev. 3:7). Therefore, we should pray to the Lord that in His sovereign grace, He will open wide the doors of opportunity so that we can make Christ known to others.

We all have the opportunity to open doors for others through our prayers. You can open doors for me and I can open doors for you as we pray for each other. You may be thousands of miles from where I am, but your prayers can change my ministry, and my prayers can change your ministry wherever you happen to be. Geography is no barrier when the Lord is involved. By prayer we can change the world without ever leaving our living room.

Doors are waiting to be opened everywhere. Some are in crowded urban neighborhoods, offices, and schools. Some are found in apartment buildings or on college campuses. Others are located in Muslim, Buddhist, or Hindu countries. Some doors are marked "closed," but they wait to be opened by the power of God. Would you join me in praying for God to open doors for the Word to go forth in conquering power? Let this be our prayer: "O God, blow the door off the hinges in Albania, Syria, Libya, Saudi Arabia, Uganda, Japan, China. And while You're at it, Lord, blow open the doors in my own town!"

From our knees we can impact distant lands. We may never preach, but our prayers may make the preaching of others successful. We may never be foreign missionaries, but our prayers may open doors for missionaries around the world. By prayer we partner with God's people everywhere. And we do that even when we never leave our home.

By prayer I can minister in Bangladesh even though I have never set foot there. By prayer I can visit Singapore, Seoul, Beijing, Tokyo, Manila, Johannesburg, Nairobi, Kiev, Sucre, Buenos Aires, Lagos, Bangalore, Madrid, Berlin, Caracas, Moscow, Hong Kong, Bangkok, Sao Paulo, Mexico City, Accra, Ankara, Baghdad, Tel Aviv, Paris, Helsinki, and a thousand other cities in countries I may never personally visit.

No terrorist threat can ground my plane; no color-coded terror alert can change my plans, no fears of war can stop me; no visa problems can keep me from my appointed visits. By prayer I can go anytime, anywhere to support the work of God.

The Second Request: Speedy Deliverance

This request may seem unexpected: "And pray that we may be delivered from wicked and evil men, for not everyone has faith" (2 Thess. 3:2). Some people will do anything to stop the good news of Jesus Christ, even to the point of violence. Not everyone is happy that you are a Christian. Not everyone is glad that your life has changed. Not everyone applauds when you speak up for Jesus. Some people want you to sit down and shut up. The "wicked and evil men" were the opponents who chased Paul out of Thessalonica and hounded his steps in every city he entered so that he was hindered from preaching the gospel. Later they succeeded in having him thrown in jail in Rome. Paul cared little for his own safety or comfort, but he was passionately concerned about the progress of the gospel.

These first two requests often go together. When we commit ourselves to be bold for Jesus, we are bound to face opposition. If you ever decide to become bold about your faith, someone is bound to object. "A great door for effective work has opened to me, and there are many who oppose me" (1 Cor. 16:9).

Open doors and adversaries generally go together. During a trip to Pittsburgh, I was standing in front of my hotel, waiting to be taken to a TV station for an interview. A man I did not know came out of the hotel and asked, "Are you going to Cornerstone TV?"

"Yes, I am." He was a pleasant fellow and we chatted for a bit, but I wasn't paying much attention because I was looking for the man who was supposed to pick us up.

Then he said, "My daughter is Miss America."

Well, that got my attention. I told him, "You could live a lifetime and never have anyone say to you, 'My daughter is Miss America.'" A few months earlier, I had read some stories about his daughter having some trouble with the Miss America organization because she wanted to speak out in favor of abstinence, but some powerful officials didn't want her to do that. Too controversial, they said.

"Is that true?" I asked. "Absolutely," he told me. The pressure on her to compromise her values had been incredible. She was an outspoken Christian who stood up for what she believed. During the interview process before she was chosen, she gave an answer to a question that emphasized her Christian faith. A woman declared, "If you keep on answering questions like that, I promise you that you'll never be Miss America." To which she replied, "It doesn't matter whether or not I'm Miss America. This is what I believe and no one is going to silence me." The woman didn't bother her anymore.

Her father told me that despite the opposition, the outpouring of support from young people had been incredible. Young people want to hear about abstinence and they want to hear about her faith. At the end of a presentation to a high school in Gary, Indiana, they asked her to sing a song. She asked if they would like to hear the operatic aria she sang in the competition or would they prefer "Amazing Grace"? They wanted to hear "Amazing Grace," so she sang it. When she finished, students and teachers joined in a standing ovation.

The Third Request: Growing Confidence

"But the Lord is faithful, and he will strengthen and protect you from the evil one. We have confidence in the Lord that you are doing and will continue to do the things we command" (2 Thess. 3:3–4). This request is very simple: Ask for growing confidence in God that He will give you everything you need when you need it. And that the Lord will be faithful to His people just as He has been faithful to you.

It all goes back to your view of God. Awhile back someone asked me what I would preach on if I had only ten sermons left to preach. I thought about it for a moment and said, "I don't know about all ten, but I know one of them would be about God's sovereignty." The person who asked the question looked at me as if to say, "That's an odd comment," but nothing is more basic than the confidence that our God is sovereign over every detail of the universe. You will have what you need when you need it. Why? Because God is faithful. Pray for growing confidence so that when trouble comes, you will still believe that God is faithful.

The Fourth Request: Undiscouraged Love

Paul says it plainly in 2 Thessalonians 3:5: "May the Lord direct your hearts into God's love." As I thought about the love of God, I wondered what adjective should go with it. As I pondered that question, the "un-" words kept coming to mind. Pray for undiminished love, undivided love, unhindered love, unconditional love. Finally, my mind settled on a word I don't think I've ever used before. *Pray for undiscouraged love.*

When trouble comes, it is so easy to become discouraged. And it's easy to become selfish and self-centered. If you are sick, it's hard to think about anything else or anyone else. When you have a family crisis or a crisis at work, it's natural to spend all your energy focused on the crisis and to spend little time or energy thinking of those around you. In moments like that, we can become inward-looking and extremely selfish so that all we want to do is talk about our own problems, our own issues, our own struggles. But what a blessing to have undiscouraged love that reaches out to others when it might be easier to crawl into a cave and have a pity party. God's love never gives up, never gives in, never loses hope, never stops reaching out. In the time of trouble, pray that His love will fill your heart.

The Fifth Request: Cheerful Perseverance

This is the last part of 2 Thessalonians 3:5: "May the Lord direct your hearts into God's love and Christ's perseverance." Fascinating phrase: Christ's perseverance. In what sense did Christ persevere? How about this from 1 Peter 2:23: "When they hurled their insults at him, he did not retaliate; when he suffered, he made no threats. Instead, he entrusted himself to him who judges justly." But what about the "cheerful" part? Where does that come from? Listen to the words of Hebrews 12:2: "Let us fix our eyes on Jesus, the author and perfecter of our faith, who for the joy set before him endured the cross, scorning its shame, and sat down at the right hand of the throne of God."

In case that isn't clear, here's how Eugene Peterson paraphrases it, "Keep your eyes on Jesus, who both began and finished this race we're in. Study how he did it. Because he never lost sight of where he was headed—that exhilarating finish in and with God—he could put up with anything along the way: cross, shame, whatever. And now he's there, in the place of honor, right alongside God" (THE MESSAGE). I like that phrase: "he never lost sight of where he was headed." He knew He was bringing salvation to the world and would soon be with His Father in heaven again. Therefore, He could put up with anything along the way.

Praying for cheerful perseverance means praying that you will never lose sight of the big picture, that you will always remember where you are going. If you have that perspective, you can endure anything. To be a Christian is to suffer. That is not the full truth of the Christian life, but it is part of it, and it is one that modern Christians sometimes resist. Today it is popular to talk about Jesus as the One who solves our problems, improves our self-image, and, above all, makes us happy. Sometimes the gospel is presented as if Jesus is the ticket to the good life. And it is true that our Lord said, "I have come that they may have life, and have it to the full" (John 10:10b). First Thessalonians 5:16 instructs us to "be joyful always." But that abundance and that joy can never be separated from the truth that to be a Christian is to suffer.

The Christians in China understand all about this. To publicly admit that you are a Christian means putting yourself, your career, and your family at risk. If you go to an unregistered church, you can be arrested for being part of an illegal gathering. During a visit to Beijing, we were warned over and over again to be careful about what we said. I met a young man from southern China who became a Christian last year through the influence of some Christians he met. That young man was so filled with joy and peace. When I asked someone if he was a Christian, I was told, "He is like-minded." That's safer than saying the "C" word.

We spent ten days in Beijing and had a wonderful time. We greatly enjoyed our time in China, and we loved meeting the Chinese people. It was an honor to be there. But there is another side to the story. In a city of thirteen million people (millions more if you count the larger region), you can find almost no evidence of religion. During our visit, we didn't see any church buildings at all. The guidebooks speak of a few historic church buildings, but they are few and far between. We didn't see any. Imagine Chicago or Philadelphia or New Orleans or New York City with no churches, or just a few. Imagine a society where religion is not discussed in public. And imagine a society where you are not free to voice criticism of the government. In America we talk endlessly about politics and religion. We argue about the impact of the "values voters" and how faith does or does not influence our leaders. As divided as America may be, at least we are free to voice our opinions.

I spoke with a Chinese man who said, "You work for the church. That is good." Then he said, "You are a priest?" No time for technicalities, I said yes. "And your son, he is a priest?" I said yes again. "Ah, father and son doing the same thing. That is good." As we walked along, he said to me, "Religion is good. A nation needs religion because religion teaches you what is right and wrong." In America we tend to make a difference between "religion" and Christianity, but in China it's safer to say *religion* than to use the "C" word. He told me that he believes "religion" is good for a nation because religion provides a moral foundation. China needs that foundation, he said, and it does not have it today.

"I have a Bible in Chinese and English and I read it," he told me. "The State cannot tell you what to believe in your heart. And if the State says, 'Don't go to church,' you can have church in your home." He folded his hands and touched his heart as he spoke those words. I think he was telling me he was "like-minded" also. Life is not easy for Christians in China. Those who are too outspoken suffer for their faith. But the Chinese church fully understands that to be a follower of Jesus means that you will suffer. It is through suffering that we become like our Lord. This is how we grow in our faith.

SEMPER FI!

When President Bush spoke to the Marines at Camp LeJeune, North Carolina, on April 3, 2000, he ended his talk with the words, "Semper Fi," the shortened version of the Marine Corps motto: "Always faithful." That should be our motto as well: "Semper Fi." Always faithful to the Lord. Always faithful to our calling. Always faithful to our family. When you know where you are going, you can be "always faithful" to the very end.

Hugh Latimer was a Protestant preacher in England in the 1500s. When Queen Mary ("Bloody Mary") came to the throne, she attempted to return England to the Roman Catholic Church. Latimer protested and was thrown into jail along with his friend Nicholas Ridley. Convicted of heresy, they were sentenced to be burned at the stake. The sentence was carried out on October 16, 1555. As they approached the stake, Ridley drew back in fear. Latimer comforted his friend with words that have echoed across the generations: "Be of good cheer, Master Ridley, and play the man, for we shall this day light such a candle in England as I trust by God's grace shall never be put out." And so they did light a candle for God by their fiery ordeal. This is cheerful perseverance. Semper Fi—Always Faithful.

IN YOU AND THROUGH YOU

As I thought about 2 Thessalonians 3 and what it means for us today, two application statements came to mind. These help us understand why Paul prayed as he did. First, what happens *to* us is not as important as what happens *in* us. We can't do much about what happens to us. Sometimes bad things happen no matter how hard we try to avoid them. Sometimes people turn against us for no reason at all. And occasionally evil people try to destroy us. In a fallen world, bad things happen to good people all the time. This passage reminds us that God is not nearly as concerned about what happens to us as He is with what happens in us. When hard times come, will we be courageous? Will we trust in God? Will we reach out in love? Will we hold on cheerfully?

In the devastating forest fires that swept through Yellowstone National Park in 1988, tens of thousands of acres were transformed into blackened ashes. Whole forests disappeared overnight. Yet today the new growth is flourishing, and the signs of the fire are disappearing. This is a parable of the Christian life. We all must go through the fire sooner or later. God allows hard times to come so that we might flourish with the new growth of Christlike character. If you are in the fire right now, ask God to do His work so that you will be more like Jesus when the trial is finally over.

Second, what happens *to* you is not as important as what happens *through* you. Paul does not always pray that troubles might cease, but he does pray for strength on the inside, growing love, increasing discernment, and a fruitful life that brings great glory to God. In this passage he prayed for speedy deliverance from his adversaries. Why is that? Paul's concern was not for himself. He was totally committed to sharing the gospel with as many people as possible. He didn't care whether he lived or died; he only wanted to make sure that others heard about Jesus. Since they were opposing his gospel preaching, he asked God to put a stop to their opposition.

This brings us to a huge point: What happens through you has a powerful impact on those around you. The people of the world watch Christians to see how we will respond when hard times come. Unsaved people pay attention to our response to trouble. They want to know if what we believe makes any difference when hard times come. Let me apply this personally. Parents, your children watch to see how you handle the problems in your marriage. They watch to see how you handle financial difficulties and trouble with other people. Your children may not say a word, but they watch and listen and learn from everything you do and say. You preach by the way you respond in a crisis.

Christian, your friends at work are watching you. Your students are watching you. Your colleagues are watching you. Your close friends are watching you. People you barely know are watching you. Your neighbors are watching you.

And from the shadows of sin and the darkness of life without Christ, lost people are watching you. They form lasting judgments by the way you handle yourself when trouble pays a visit to your home. Will you give in to bitterness? Will you lose your temper? Will you become selfish, moody, withdrawn? Will you drift away from your faith altogether? Or will you respond with courage, hope, faith, love, and God-inspired cheerfulness? The words of Edgar Guest come to mind:

I'd rather see a sermon than hear one any day;

I'd rather one should walk with me than merely tell the way.

The eye's a better pupil and more willing than the ear;

Fine counsel is confusing, but example's always clear;

And the best of all the preachers are the men who live their creeds,

For to see good put in action is what everybody needs.

You preach a sermon by the way you respond in the time of trouble. Paul knew that. That's why he asked others to pray for him, and that's why he prayed like this for others. I end where I began. Prayer is our greatest weapon, our most powerful resource. Use it and you can change the course of history. Use it and God will open blinded eyes that they might see the light of the gospel. Use it and God will raise the spiritually dead and give them new life in Christ. Use it and your children will grow strong in the Lord, your friends will find new courage, your church will gain new power, your pastor will be given new blessing, and you will grow in Christ.

Paul prayed for effective proclamation, speedy deliverance, growing confidence, undiscouraged love, and cheerful perseverance.

Pray like this every day. And then stand back and see what God will do.

SEVEN

FORWARD-LEANING DEFENSE

"There is no victory at bargain basement prices."

—**GENERAL DWIGHT EISENHOWER**

"WORLD WAR IV BEGAN IN A LONG string of terrorist attacks, whose real nature went unrecognized until on September 11, 2001, huge billows of black smoke curled above New York City, Washington, D.C., and a field near Gettysburg, Pennsylvania."[1] So begins a speech delivered on November 19, 2004, by Michael Novak, former U.S. Ambassador to the U.N. Human Rights Commission. While some will argue about the Roman numerals, everyone agrees that the 9/11 attacks changed the strategic face of the world. For the first time, terms like asymmetric warfare, rogue nuclear states, bioterrorism, anthrax attacks, and sleeper cells entered the common vocabulary. Soon we were to learn about IED (Improvised Explosive Devices) that would take many American lives in Iraq. Later the world would be introduced to suicide subway bombers and explosives hidden in shoes. Not long ago we added liquid explosives to the list.

Michael Novak points out that this new kind of warfare calls for new strategies. The strategy of Mutually Assured Destruction that worked for years during the Cold War doesn't work in the twenty-first century. Osama bin Laden explained the fundamental difference between the Islamic terrorists and the nations of the West this way: "We love death. Americans love life. This is the difference between us."[2]

How do you fight against a shadowy enemy you can't even see, who doesn't play by the normal rules of warfare, and whose deepest values run counter to those taken for granted by civilized people? Novak argues for what he calls "forward-leaning defense." That's a new name for an old concept. Sometimes the best defense is a good offense. Perhaps a football analogy will help. Some teams play a "bend-but-don't-break defense." That means you give up yards in the middle of the field and either play for a turnover, hope the offense makes a mistake, or stiffen inside your own twenty-yard line. That may be good defense in football, but it is disastrous when facing an enemy who views his own violent death as the pathway to paradise.

What does it mean for the Christian to practice forward-leaning defense? Satan fights his dirty war using many different weapons. Consider the following. "Pastor Ray, what do I do when those thoughts come to me?" the young man asked. He was in his late thirties, a rising young executive, by all outward appearances the very image of success. Almost ten years ago he took his MBA degree and parlayed it into a profitable career as a stockbroker. He has a good job, is well-respected by his peers, and seems to have no trouble mixing his faith and his work. What could be wrong?

As a single man in a high-powered business environment, he faces numerous temptations, many coming from the sexual arena. "I've asked God to give me a Christian wife, but He hasn't answered that prayer yet. Sometimes my mind is filled with thoughts that embarrass me. And sometimes I give in to the temptation I feel." If you change the name or a few details, it was a story I had heard many times before. In fact, the story is as old as the Bible itself. Temptation is the same for us as it was for Adam and Eve in the garden of Eden. Satan tempts us today in the same way he tempted Jesus in the wilderness. From the very beginning a battle has raged for the souls of men and women, a battle that touches all of us sooner or later.[3]

IT'S NOT A SIN
TO BE TEMPTED

Perhaps the place to begin is with the important truth that *it is not a sin to be tempted*. Many Christians feel needless guilt because they have equated temptation with sin. Yet we know that our Lord was tempted and was without sin (Heb. 4:15). Was the temptation real? The answer must be yes. But if the sinless Son of God could be tempted, then temptation itself cannot be sinful.

Temptation is a sign that we still live in a fallen world. It's not the temptation that matters; it's how you respond to it.

Think how many temptations you and I face in an ordinary day. Staying in bed late—the temptation to laziness. Dressing carelessly—the temptation to sloppiness. Growling at the breakfast table—the temptation to unkindness. Arguing over who should change the baby this time—the temptation to selfishness. Starting work ten minutes late—the temptation to slothfulness. Losing your temper when a coworker crashes your computer—the temptation to impatience. Flirting with that good looking woman, or taking a second look at that good-looking man—the temptation to lust. Refusing to speak to a person who has hurt you—the temptation to malice. Repeating a juicy story of your neighbor's misfortune—the temptation to gossip. Taking a secret drink at a party—the temptation to drunkenness. Lying awake at night thinking sensual thoughts—the temptation to impurity. Taking your anger out on the children after a hard day—the temptation to cruelty. Going out to eat when you can't afford it—the temptation to self-indulgence. Having a second helping and then a third—the temptation to gluttony. Firing off a hasty letter to a friend who hurt you—the temptation to revenge.

The Danger Within

That list could be expanded almost infinitely. We do well to remember that temptation is never remote but is a part of the life of every one of us. James 1:14–15 reminds us that "temptation comes from our own desires, which entice us and drag us away. These desires give birth to sinful actions. And when sin is allowed to grow, it gives birth to death" (NLT). Even though you are a Christian, the principle of sin within you will remain till the day you die. It doesn't really help to say, "The devil made me do it," though he is the diabolical mastermind working behind the scenes. Temptation is not merely something external, something "out there" that lures us into sin. Temptation arises from within us as our evil desires produce evil actions that lead to spiritual death.

One major problem we face is that temptation comes when we least expect it. If we could schedule our temptations, we'd do much better. "I've decided to fight temptation next Saturday afternoon at 4 p.m.," we would say. Unfortunately temptation often shows up unannounced at 9:30 Wednesday morning. It comes when our guard is down and we are most prone to give in.

That leads to a second important truth: While temptation itself is not sinful, yielding to temptation is. We are born with a tendency to sin. The Bible itself bears witness that the best men and women faced temptation and often fell. Eve ate the fruit and then gave it to Adam, who joined her in rebellion against God. Abraham lied about his wife. Sarah lied to God. Lot compromised in Sodom. Jacob was born cheating. Moses struck the rock in defiant anger. Elijah complained against God. David committed adultery and then had a man murdered to cover it up. Jonah ran away from God. Peter denied the Lord. John Mark deserted Paul. The Bible is filled with stories of men and women who faced temptation and were defeated by it. These facts should not discourage us, but rather cause us to seriously consider our own spiritual condition. What happened to them may happen to us.

Positive Uses of Temptation

God is able to use even the worst temptation to bring us to the place where we will begin to grow spiritually. When Joseph ran away from Potiphar's wife (Gen. 39), he ended up in jail, but the whole experience produced in him the strength of character that prepared him to become the second most important ruler in Egypt. When we resist, we actually grow stronger.

Every temptation—whether large or small—requires a moment-by-moment decision. When your boss asks you to fudge the figures on the monthly financial report, you only have a few seconds to decide how to respond. When you are surfing the Internet and happen to run across a site filled with pornography, you must choose immediately whether or not you'll click the mouse button. Sometimes you will have to bite your tongue, and then bite it again to keep from sinning.

Or you'll just have to learn how to say no.

The lady is single, attractive, and in her late fifties. She has been a widow for almost fifteen years. When a male friend began showing interest in her, she was both flattered and pleased. After several months he suggested that they take a trip together to a seaside resort. Of course, he said, we'll have to sleep in the same room in order to save money. He was offended when she politely told him no, thanks. Soon after that the budding relationship ended. Does she have any regrets? A few, mostly because she enjoyed his company and felt they shared many common interests. But she says she has no doubts about her decision to say no. What if his intentions were entirely honorable? Her answer was simple: "If you begin to compromise in small areas, soon you'll compromise in big ones."

Unseen Battles

What practical steps can we take to win those skirmishes one by one? James 4:7 commands us to submit to God and resist the devil. How do we do that on a daily basis? First, it helps enormously to live by a schedule. First Timothy 4:7 says, "Train yourself to be godly." The word *train* is a Greek word from which we get the

English word *gymnasium*. It suggests sweaty shoes, worn-out jerseys, scarred helmets, callused hands, and aching muscles. No one becomes godly by accident. You can't sleep late and lounge around like a couch potato if you want to win the prize of a godly life. And you can't indulge yourself physically, mentally, or spiritually. You're going to have to get in shape in every sense of the word. Discipline builds spiritual muscles that arm you against temptation. They make the battle winnable, but not easy.

For me personally that means getting up early so I can spend some time in the Word. It also means keeping a journal on my computer where I record my weight, my goals for the day, my observations on what God is teaching me, and a prayer for the day. I haven't always done this, and I confess there are days when I don't keep this schedule, but it seems that I have extra strength when I start the day with the Lord.

Second, you need to look at your own pattern of sin. Analyze your life. When are you most likely to experience temptation? Where? Why? What triggers it? What comes before? After? What kind of mood are you in? For some it may be during a lunch break; for others it may occur on a business trip. Or it might happen when you are extremely tired or when you are at home alone, or during the forty-five minutes before dinner when the children are cranky, or when your neighbor calls to complain about the noise your dog makes. It might happen on the weekend or while you are watching a particular TV program. For some, it may happen immediately after successfully completing a major project.

Having done that kind of analysis, it's important to cut off the feeding factors. Be ruthless. Romans 8:13 speaks of putting to death the deeds of the flesh. You must be brutal in your attack against your own tendency to sin. Many Christians fail precisely at this point because they are not tough enough on themselves. Martin Luther commented that you can't stop the birds from flying over your head, but you don't have to let them build a nest in your hair. This may mean a total reorientation of your life. For one man it meant breaking off a relationship with a young woman who was not a Christian. He found he could not date her and speak openly about his faith at the same time. After some mental agony he decided to end the relationship. "It was hard, but I'm glad I did it, because that's when I started growing spiritually," he declared.

Third, don't be ashamed to admit your weakness. God never meant for you to struggle against sin by yourself. James 5:16 says, "Confess your sins to each other and pray for each other so that you may be healed." Satan loves to keep Christians away from each other. He convinces us not to confess our sins because it will cause others to think less of us. But the opposite is almost always true.

I know a man who told a joke that seemed funny to him but was offensive to a close friend. When he called to apologize, he admitted that he often spoke quickly without thinking of the consequences. His friend not only forgave him but also asked to be held accountable because he has the same problem in dealing with his children.

It helps to have a friend who knows your weaknesses. That friend can hold you accountable by asking hard questions and refusing to accept easy answers. Sometimes we need a kick in the pants, and sometimes we need a pat on the back. A good friend will know which is appropriate.

Fourth, pray for deliverance. Jesus taught His disciples to pray, "Lead us not into temptation, but deliver us from the evil one" (Matt. 6:13). That prayer is something like this, "O Lord, there are enemies on every hand and temptations without and within. Don't let me fall into the devil's trap but deliver me from his power. Give me eyes to see the 'way of escape' and a heart ready to choose what is right." If you can't remember those words in a moment of crisis, cry out, "Help, Lord!" and He will surely answer you.

I find that if I pray immediately when I have evil thoughts, confessing to God that these thoughts are wrong, and ask Him to take them captive and make my thoughts obedient to Christ, I have victory each time.

"I'm Trying Not To"

Fifth, take the "way of escape" God gives you. First Corinthians 10:13 promises us God will never allow us to be tempted beyond what we can bear. "But when you are tempted, he will also provide a way out so that you can stand up under it." That verse is encouraging, but it must not be taken for granted. The way of escape is always there, but if not taken, it may disappear. In most situations it will not be an angel's voice but just a fleeting thought, *This is wrong. Don't do it.* Every sin is a choice to do wrong. Before you make that choice, you always have another choice. That other choice is your "way of escape."

Perhaps you've heard about the little boy who was lying under an apple tree. The farmer asked, "What are you trying to do? Steal an apple?" "No, sir, I'm trying not to," he replied. Many of us are trying not to, but we fail because we lie down under the apple tree.

In sexual temptation, the "way of escape" may only last a moment. The sad story of Samson reminds us of what happens when a man keeps making the wrong choices. It's too late to decide to do right when you wake up with your head in Delilah's lap. At that point his doom was sealed. The same thing happens to any of us when we let our emotions drive our decisions. But for a moment, before you put the pedal to the metal and go wild, the way of escape is always there. That's why the Bible tells us to "flee from sexual immorality" (1 Cor. 6:18) and "flee the evil desires of youth" (2 Tim. 2:22).

When we repeatedly give in to temptation, something deadly begins to happen. Sin builds a certain force in our lives that is difficult to overcome. The Bible speaks of a seared conscience (1 Tim. 4:2). When that happens, the choice to do wrong becomes progressively easier. The "way of escape" is always there; you simply do not see it any longer. That is the danger of saying yes when you ought to say no. An ingrained pattern of wrongdoing cannot easily be changed. That's why it's crucial to say no to temptation the very first time.

Sixth, memorize the Word of God. Psalm 119:11 says, "I have

hidden your word in my heart that I might not sin against you." Jesus prayed, "Make them holy by your truth; teach them your word, which is truth" (John 17:17 NLT). The Word of God not only tells us how to live; it also provides the power we need to make the right choices.

A young man came to see me because he had been struggling to keep his thought life pure. Though he was bold about his faith on the job, he felt utterly defeated because of his ongoing struggles in the area of moral purity. He said, "I want to be married someday, but how can I be a Christian husband when I'm not the man I want to be right now?" As I talked to him, I sensed two things that gave me hope—his utter honesty and a deep-seated desire to do whatever it took to put his life on a new course. I challenged him to begin memorizing Scripture. He seemed skeptical that it would make any difference, and I told him that his life would not change overnight. He asked where he should begin.

I suggested starting with Psalm 119, the longest chapter in the Bible—176 verses. It's all about the power of God's Word. Not many people would have the courage to tackle such a huge project, and fewer still would finish. But I suspected that this young man was different. He left my office with a promise that he would start and that he would check in with me from time to time. Over the next few weeks, when I saw him in church I asked him how he was doing. That was during the spring. When summer came, he volunteered to serve at a Christian camp. He told me that he planned to continue memorizing.

I think it took him ten full months to memorize all of Psalm 119. Finally the day came when he sat in my office and said, "Check me out." I sat and followed along in my Bible as he recited all 176 verses. It was an amazing experience for me to hear this young man recite God's Word with so much confidence and so much joy. Something had clearly happened inside his heart as the Word had taken root. From time to time, he stopped and commented on how powerful this verse was or how much that verse meant to him or what amazing truth this verse contained.

Clearly he had memorized more than words on paper. The life-giving Word of God had entered his soul. And all that Psalm 119 promises had come true in his life. He quite simply was not the defeated man who walked into my office ten months earlier. The Word had done its work. That was a few years ago. He continued to memorize Scripture. Today he is married to a wonderful Christian woman, and together they are raising their family for the Lord. He would say that memorizing Scripture changed his life.

Seventh, remember that the Holy Spirit lives in you. If Jesus were visibly beside us, how would we act? What would we say? What would we watch? Where would we not go? The problem is that He is not visibly with us, so we feel free to do what we want without visible restraint. But we need to realize that the Holy Spirit is inside us, indwelling us. We are His home, His temple (1 Cor. 6:19–20). So wherever we go, we are taking Him along with us; what we watch, we watch through the eyes of His dwelling place; what we say issues from His home; when we are rude and obnoxious, He is suffering the indignity of such action coming from where He lives.

THE SON OF GOD AIDS US WHEN WE ARE TEMPTED

One final thought will help us in the hour of temptation. Hebrews 12:2 tells us to "fix our eyes on Jesus." Take a long look at the Son of God who struggled in the wilderness and won the victory over the devil. If He won the battle, so can we, because His divine power is available to us today.

As I have shared these principles with many people, they have discovered that God is indeed as good as His Word. He will never allow us to be tempted beyond our limits. I have seen the weakest Christians triumph over the Goliaths of life through His power.

Temptation is the common experience of the people of God. We will never escape it as long as we live in a fallen world. But God has given us everything we need to win the battle every time.

EIGHT

SINGING
YOUR WAY
TO VICTORY

"I have no use for cranks who despise music, because it is a gift of God. Music drives away the Devil and makes people happy; they forget thereby all wrath, unchastity, arrogance, and the like. Next after theology, I give to music the highest place and the greatest honor."
—MARTIN LUTHER

"AFTER CONSULTING THE PEOPLE, Jehoshaphat appointed men to sing to the LORD and to praise him for the splendor of his holiness as they went out at the head of the army, saying: 'Give thanks to the LORD, for his love endures forever'" (2 Chron. 20:21).

This must be the most unusual battle plan in history. The year: 850 B.C. The place: Jerusalem. The king: a godly man named Jehoshaphat. He was a good king, and he reigned during a period of prosperity and happiness for the people of Judah. God smiled upon him because he was a man of the Book. He honored God's Word, and God honored him in return.

All of that changed when word came that a vast enemy army was approaching from the southeast. They came from Edom on the other side of the Dead Sea. When the king got the news, the advancing army was only forty miles away and closing rapidly. Obviously the Moabites, the Ammonites, and the Meunites had planned their attack for many weeks. The danger was very real. When forty messengers gave the king the bad news, they told him that the army was coming "against you" (2 Chron. 20:2), meaning Jehoshaphat now faced a very personal crisis. The army he faced was far larger than the army he commanded. In a straightforward battle, the men of Judah would lose badly. This wasn't a fair fight.

What will Jehoshaphat do?

A person's response in the time of crisis tells a great deal about his character. Our first reaction reveals our deepest values. We may cover up a problem, we may deny it, we may panic and throw in the towel, or we may decide to turn to the Lord.

Jehoshaphat responded in three ways (2 Chron. 20:3): First, he took the threat seriously. Second, he prayed to the Lord. Third, he called for a fast.

CHRIST-CENTERED, TEAM-ORIENTED, BATTLE-FOCUSED

Second Chronicles 20:4 says that from all over Judah people came to Jerusalem to seek the Lord together. Because their leader felt the burden, the people shared the burden with him. Everything in this story turns on this simple point. When the king issued a call, the people came to seek the Lord together. Recently I ran across a Web site for an organization called Battle-Focused Ministries. Their model for spiritual warfare is "Christ-centered, team-oriented, and battle-focused." They explain the second principle this way:

Most popular spiritual warfare instruction focuses on the individual Christian's personal struggle with the weaknesses of his own flesh and his egocentric spiritual battle against demons, and promises deliverance from the weariness of the conflict. That is in stark contrast to the training a soldier receives in our nation's armed forces. Although each individual soldier must be trained to survive on a battlefield, the vast majority of his training concerns accomplishing the mission, defeating an enemy, by fighting as a member of a team under the orders of his chain of command.[1]

Jehoshaphat understood that by himself, he could not defeat the mighty Ammonite army; but united together with his people, they could multiply their prayers to the Lord of Hosts. With the people assembled around him, and the enemy army advancing hour by hour, Jehoshaphat offers one of the greatest prayers in the Bible. He begins by declaring God's greatness: "O LORD, God of our fathers, are you not the God who is in heaven? You rule over all the kingdoms of the nations. Power and might are in your hand, and no one can withstand you" (2 Chron. 20:6). Next, he reminds God of the promises He made to take care of His people when they were in trouble. Then he tells God, "We're in big trouble now!" He freely admits, "We have no power to face this vast army that is attacking us" (v. 12). And he concludes with this simple confession: "We do not know what to do, but our eyes are upon you" (v. 12).

We tend to get all mixed up about prayer, don't we? We look at the externals—the form, the words, and the length. But God looks at the internals—faith, sincerity, honesty, and humility. Jehoshaphat's prayer proves that in a moment of crisis, a short prayer often means much more than a long prayer. Because his prayer came from a heart of faith, it got God's attention in a big way.

Go to the Gorge

When the prayer was over, the Holy Spirit prompted a man named Jahaziel to stand up and announce the battle plan:

This is what the LORD says to you: "Do not be afraid or discouraged because of this vast army. For the battle is not yours, but God's. Tomorrow march down against them. They will be climbing up by the Pass of Ziz, and you will find them at the

*end of the gorge in the Desert of Jeruel. You will not have to
fight this battle. Take up your positions; stand firm and see the
deliverance the LORD will give you, O Judah and Jerusalem. Do
not be afraid; do not be discouraged. Go out to face them tomorrow, and the LORD will be with you."* (2 Chron. 20:15–17)

God gave them three specific details: (1) A time: tomorrow. (2) A
place: the end of the gorge. (3) A plan: Stand firm and see the
deliverance the Lord will give you. And He said it very plainly, "You
will not have to fight this battle." It doesn't get any clearer than
that. Go out, take your positions, and then don't move a muscle.
Stand still and watch God do the work.

Singing . . . Loudly!

Satan's greatest weapon against us is discouragement. If he can
cause us to give up, he wins before the battle even starts. The real
question becomes, Will you go in your own strength or in the
strength of the Lord? If the battle is yours, you are in big trouble.
If the battle is ours, we are in big trouble. If the battle is the Lord's,
we are going to be OK.

The Levites began to worship the Lord loudly (2 Chron. 20:19).
These were the trained temple singers who had first been appointed
in David's day. Across the generations they had led the people of
God in public worship.

Now they began to sing . . . loudly!

This is not a small point.

Remember the situation. The bad guys are closing fast on
Jerusalem. The odds don't favor the men of Judah. The king has
just proclaimed, "We do not know what to do." Jahaziel has just
said, "Stand still and see the salvation of the Lord" (v. 17 NKJV).
What happens next? The singers begin to sing . . . loudly!

Luther said it very plainly: "Music drives away the Devil and
makes people happy; they forget thereby all wrath, unchastity,
arrogance, and the like." Do you believe music drives the devil
away? I do.

Preaching is one thing. Prayer is one thing. But music is something else. *It touches the heart and soul at a level too deep for words.* Music is not better than preaching or better than prayer, but music takes the words of the sermon and brings them home to the heart, and music lifts our spirit to believe the words we bravely utter in prayer.

Invading the Devil's Territory

Music is a weapon of spiritual warfare. And the devil hates it when we sing worship to God. He hates our music because our singing rouses our souls, gives us courage, lifts our hearts, restores our faith, builds our confidence, unites our voices, and lifts up the name of the Lord like a mighty banner.

Music is not just preparation for warfare. Music *is* spiritual warfare. When God's people sing together, we invade the devil's territory.

What happens the next day is actually very simple. Jehoshaphat sends his army out to do battle with the enemy. We all know that a wise general puts his best troops at the front so they will bear the brunt of the battle. So this is what the king did: "After consulting the people, Jehoshaphat appointed men to sing to the LORD and to praise him for the splendor of his holiness as they went out at the head of the army, saying: 'Give thanks to the LORD, for his love endures forever'" (2 Chron. 20:21). He put the male singers at the front of the army and had them lead the way to the battlefront. And he had them sing as the army marched along, thus giving up the element of surprise.

> *As they began to sing and praise, the LORD set ambushes against the men of Ammon and Moab and Mount Seir who were invading Judah, and they were defeated. The men of Ammon and Moab rose up against the men from Mount Seir to destroy and annihilate them. After they finished slaughtering the men from Seir, they helped to destroy one another.* (2 Chron. 20:22–23)

Note the key phrase, "As they began to sing and praise." *It was their singing that unleashed the ambush that led to the rout of the enemy army.* The slaughter was so great that it took three days to collect the plunder from the battlefield. When that was done, the people gathered in the Valley of Beracah for a praise service. Then they returned to Jerusalem, singing and praising as they went to the temple.

The Doxology and the Devil

You can't escape the implication of the text. Music played a vital role in this amazing victory. Music is not just a means of praising God. It is also a means of throwing the devil and his cohorts into confusion. John Piper points out that "God has appointed the use of spiritual songs as an effective weapon against his archenemy Satan."[2]

Mary Schlosser worked for years as a missionary in China. She used to say, "I sing the doxology and dismiss the devil." Amy Carmichael, missionary to India, said, "I believe truly that Satan cannot endure it and so slips out of the room—more or less—when there is a true song."

In my pastoral ministry, on many occasions I went to church on Sunday morning feeling weak and tired. Perhaps it was because of a busy week, or perhaps I was carrying a particular burden. Sometimes my mind would be going in a thousand different directions. And then the worship service would begin. It might be with the mighty pipe organ playing "Come, Thou Almighty King," or it might be with the worship band leading "How Great Is Our God" or "Blessed Be Your Name" or "Indescribable." Or it might be singing "Like a River Glorious" or "Down at the Cross" or "Guide Me, O Thou Great Jehovah," or perhaps it was a new worship chorus I was learning for the first time. I have had this amazing experience over and over again. As the congregation worshiped, my mind cleared, my doubts departed, my worries receded, my faith swelled, and my heart was lifted to heaven. When the time came to preach, the Holy Spirit came in great power. This has happened so many times that I cannot believe it was by chance.

Let the Pastors Sing

If we want spiritual victory over the devil, one way to get it is to sing our way there. I find it noteworthy that the people of God were singing before, during, and after the battle. They ambushed the enemy with music. We should do the same thing.

Let the pastors sing. Let the elders sing. Let the deacons sing. Let the old folks sing. Let the young people sing. Let the children sing.

Fill your heart with God-honoring music all day long. C. J. Mahaney says that we ought to listen every day to music that focuses on the cross of Christ. I think that's a wonderful idea. Given today's resources, there is no reason that every Christian cannot go through each day listening to God-centered, Christ-exalting music.

You can find it on the Internet. You can play it on a CD. You can play it on your iPod. You can play it on a cassette tape. You can listen on your Walkman. You can listen to Christian music on the radio. You can buy a DVD of Christian music. You can write your own music. You can buy a hymnbook.

When you are discouraged, sing "Shout to the Lord." When you feel like quitting, sing "Great Is Thy Faithfulness." When you feel empty, sing "Come Thou Fount." When you are tempted, sing "How Great Thou Art." When you feel overwhelmed with guilt, sing "Wonderful, Merciful Savior." When you are hungry to know God better, sing "As the Deer."

Parents, sing to your children . . . and to your grandchildren. Make sure they hear you singing in church. Teach your children and grandchildren to sing hymns, gospel songs, and choruses.

Sing while you are in the shower. Sing while you ride your bike. Sing along while you listen to the radio. Sing while you work out.

Men, sing together . . . loudly! Women, sing together . . . joyfully! Children, sing together . . . spontaneously!

Drive the Devil Nuts

Here's something else I've been thinking about. If we want to take on the devil, we need to take our music outside the four walls of the church. We've heard about "Prayer Walks." How about some Praise Walks where the body of Christ comes together to sing publicly? Black churches often understand the power of praise better than white churches do, and some of them hold some summer services outdoors where the people's praise can fill the neighborhood and serve notice to the devil that God's people are meeting for worship. How about churches meeting in parks for public praise services? If the devil gets his music played everywhere, why shouldn't we be at least as bold about taking God's music to the streets? A little creative thought will suggest dozens of ways we can sing the Lord's praises out where the people are.

Before next Sunday, take time to prepare your heart by listening to God-honoring music. Ask God to enable you to worship Him joyfully when you go to church. And when the congregation stands and the organ plays, the band starts, the words flash on the screen, or you pick up a hymnbook, don't hold back. Sing with all your heart and soul and mind and strength.

Go ahead. Drive the devil nuts. Keep on singing and drive him away. He hates the music God loves. Satan hates a singing church. So sing out and make the devil mad.

One final word. I add this because we live in a day when music has become a contentious issue in many churches. For the last couple of decades we've heard a great deal about "worship wars" that have torn apart many local congregations. Instead of using music to fight the devil, we've used music as a weapon to fight each other. How sad. How tragic. How Satan must crow over our divisive attitudes. Ask God to deliver you from musical smugness.

As I have traveled the world, I have learned that God's people worship Him in a bewildering variety of styles, languages, accents, and rhythms. When we look down on others whose musical tastes differ from our own, we run the risk of destroying the unity of the body of Christ. We don't all worship the same way, and that's OK.

But we do worship the same Lord. And it's in His name that we will win our battle with the devil. Keep the main thing the main thing, and all will be well.

Singing will bring new strength to your spiritual walk. Singing will bring new power to your spiritual warfare. Singing will build up your faith. Singing will strengthen the whole church of God.

God loves it and the devil hates it when you sing for the glory of God. Sing out . . . and you will see the salvation of the Lord.

NINE

CATACLYSMIC TIMES: SPIRITUAL WARFARE IN THE LAST DAYS

"The earth will be the scene of the final triumph of Christ and his church and the scene of Satan's final defeat. It is the dust of this earth that shall season Satan's diet forever."

—DONALD GREY BARNHOUSE

WE DO LIVE IN STRANGE TIMES. Someone has called this the age of anxiety, and it seems appropriate enough. Not long ago I found this headline: "Most Think Country Headed in Wrong Direction." Those words could be slightly altered to read like this: "Most Think Family Headed in Wrong Direction." "Most Think Marriage Headed in Wrong Direction." "Most Think Career Headed in Wrong Direction." "Most Think World Headed in Wrong Direction."

A few months ago I attended a worship service where the pastor said during a prayer, "It seems that we live in cataclysmic times," referring to recent earthquakes, hurricanes, and a tsunami in Asia that had left hundreds of thousands dead and millions more impoverished. I thought later of the continuing unrest in North Korea, Iran, Iraq, across the Middle East, and threats of terrorism in Europe and America.

A few days later I had lunch with a friend who is an executive working in Christian media. As we talked about recent terrorist threats, he commented that everyone in the restaurant was thinking, *When will it happen here?* The fear that "it" will happen to us has been right beneath the surface ever since 9/11. I have often thought that the national blood pressure went up about a hundred points after 9/11 and has never really come down. Our fear makes us angry, uptight, tense, hostile, sullen, and very impatient with each other. I see it on my bike rides, because when you travel city streets, you live in constant awareness that (a) drivers don't see you, (b) if they see you, they don't notice you, and (c) if they really do see you, they don't like you. So you pay close attention to the cars coming and going and often brushing right against you. I see the frustration on the faces of the drivers, and often I hear it when they honk their horns at the slightest provocation.

Lest you think I'm overstating it, the September 2005 issue of *Johns Hopkins Magazine* focused on the seven deadly sins: "Americans hate each other. There is not only the everyday empirical evidence of wrath along interstate highways, but in the snakepits of real estate, marriage, shopping, pro wrestling, and health insurance."[1] So begins the article on anger by Wayne Biddle.

He adds this trenchant observation: "Anger seems nowadays just a millionth of an inch beneath every human surface, passive or aggressive, and it will bite your head off, stab you in the back, laugh in your face, leave you twisting in the wind—maybe all at once, and more."[2]

The anger that lurks beneath the surface is a symptom of a world that seems to be spinning out of control. During lunch, my friend and I spoke of the opportunities this provides for Christians to be bold about our faith. The Bible predicts a time in the last days when God will shake the nations so that only those things that cannot be shaken will remain (Heb. 12:26–27). When Eugene Peterson paraphrased the last part of verse 27 in *The Message*, he said that God will shake the earth, "getting rid of all the historical and religious junk so that the unshakable essentials stand clear and uncluttered." Unshakable essentials. That says it all. God is shaking the earth so that we will figure out what matters most.

THE PATHS OF GLORY

In the end everything that man builds collapses before his eyes. A friend sent me an e-mail containing these lines from a poem called "Gray's Elegy" written in a country churchyard in England:

> *The boast of heraldry, the pomp of power*
> *And all that beauty, all that wealth e'er gave*
> *Awaits alike the inevitable hour*
> *The paths of glory lead but to the grave.*

According to 1 John 2:17, "The world is passing away along with its desires" (ESV). Indeed, the best and brightest of us will someday die. All that we do will eventually be forgotten.

Consider these next two sentences carefully: Those who look to this world for approval will eventually be disappointed, because the best things of this world must one day disappear. Those who look to the God who created the world will find safety and security that will last forever.

What a revelation judgment day will be for all of us. The things we thought were so important, so vital; what we included on our personal résumé; the degrees we earned, the money we made, the deals we closed, the classes we taught, the friends we cultivated in high places, the buildings we built, the organizations we managed, the budgets we balanced, the books we wrote, the songs we sang, the records we made, the trips we took, the portfolios we built, the fortunes we amassed; the positions we finally attained so that the people of the world and even our Christian friends would know that we didn't just sit on the couch watching *The Simpsons* every night— all that stuff that we take such pride in, the things that in themselves are not evil or wrong or bad, but are the "stuff" of life in this world, all of it, every single last bit of it, every part of it, considered singularly and then combined together to give us our reputation, our standing, our place in the world, even our place in the Christian world, our name in lights, our claim to fame, our reason for existence, our bragging rights, the proof that we were here and we made a name for ourselves in the short fifty or sixty or even eighty or ninety years that we have on Planet Earth, think of it! all of it added together means nothing, zip, zero, nada, vanity of vanities, all is vanity (I think I've heard that somewhere before). That's a very long sentence, isn't it? I wrote it that way to emphasize how easy it is for us to get sucked into the world's way of thinking, how quickly it happens, and on so many different levels.

All of it will someday amount to nothing.

Sometimes people hear that I'm an author and seem a bit impressed. But it doesn't amount to much in the great scheme of things. Soon after my first book came out, a friend called to say he found a copy at a garage sale for a quarter. When I asked if he bought it, he laughed and said no. So it goes. You write books that are published with great fanfare only to go out of print sooner or later and end up on some dusty bookshelf, or more likely in a garage sale, or even more likely sold for a few pennies on eBay.

Long ago I realized that my books are destined to be landfill someday. Some of them probably already are mulch in a yard in Southern California. Such is life. If this sounds melancholy, I don't mean it that way. It's just the way the universe works. Nothing lasts forever. We won't live forever on the earth. We are disposable creatures, perishable, "a flower quickly fading," here today and gone tomorrow. And we do live in cataclysmic times, in which God is shaking the world. That shaking will increase in the days to come as we near the return of Jesus Christ to the earth.

What should we expect in the days ahead? What spiritual conditions will we confront? Let's begin by looking at Paul's words in 2 Timothy 3:1–5.

THE WORLD
IN THE LAST DAYS

"But mark this: There will be terrible times in the last days" (2 Tim. 3:1). Two questions come to mind. First, what does Paul mean by the expression "last days"? That phrase has at least three meanings. It can apply to the entire period between the first and second comings of Christ. Since Christ could have come at any time, the entire church age can be called the "last days." It also applies to unique periods of spiritual testing that occur at different times in different places. Finally, it obviously applies to the last few weeks and months and years preceding our Lord's return to the earth. I find it helpful to think in terms of labor pains. A pregnant woman knows when she is about to give birth by the frequency and severity of her labor pains. In the same way, the various things that Paul lists in the first few verses of 2 Timothy 3 will always be present in some form, but will increase dramatically near the end of the age. Are we in the last days? No matter how you define it, the answer is yes. And we may indeed be living in the final days before the return of Christ to the earth.

Second, what will the "last days" be like? The word translated *terrible* occurs only here and one other place in the New Testament. In its other occurrence, it refers to the two violent men who were possessed by demons in the region of Gadara (Matt. 8:28). They were wild, uncontrollable men who lived among the tombs. The particular Greek word used to describe them is also used in 2 Timothy 3:1. The "last days" will be fierce, violent, dangerous, and frightening. Here's another way you could say it: In the last days, savage times will come as men cast off all moral restraint and society begins to disintegrate.

Raw Paganism

Two decades ago evangelical philosopher and theologian Carl Henry predicted that as America progressively loses its Judeo-Christian heritage, paganism will grow bolder. What we saw in

131

the last half of the twentieth century was a kind of benign humanism, but he predicted that by the start of the twenty-first century, we would face a situation not unlike the first century when the Christian faith confronted raw paganism—humanism with the pretty face ripped off, revealing the angry monster underneath. His words have come true, and are coming truer with every passing day. So Paul warns Timothy, "After I am gone, things are going to get worse before they get better. Buckle up, Timothy. Terrible times are coming" (see 2 Tim. 3:1). That's why Paul said, "Mark this," or "Understand this," or "Pay attention to this." Don't be naive and think that everything is going to be OK. It's not all going to be OK. But forewarned is forearmed. If we know what is going to happen, we won't be surprised when it does.

Catalogue of Corruption

The first five verses of 2 Timothy 3 offer a sobering catalogue of corruption. In a sense, this is a shorter version of Romans 1:18–32. This is what happens when a nation turns its back on God. First, there is a total rejection of God. People are unholy, ungrateful, lovers of themselves, lovers of pleasure rather than lovers of God. Second, this leads to a total moral collapse. People become lovers of money, conceited, without love toward others, boastful, proud, unforgiving, conceited, "not lovers of [what is] good." Third, the end result is the total breakdown of society. People will be treacherous, rash, slanderous, brutal, disobedient to parents, abusive, and without self-control. That last phrase means that in the end, anything goes. No rules, no moral absolutes, no restraints of any kind. Every man does that which is right in his own eyes, and woe to the person who dares to question his "lifestyle choices."

It's interesting that Paul includes "disobedient to parents." It may seem too trivial to be in such a solemn list, but for Paul, disobedience is the spark that ignites the flame that leaves the home in ashes. (Is it any wonder that divorce has become commonplace or that many people want to redefine marriage to allow homosexuals to marry each other? No, it's not surprising, and we haven't reached the bottom of the pit of moral degradation.)

In the light of Bible prophecy, we should expect that as we approach the end times, all these things will increase in intensity and frequency, until we have the situation portrayed in the book of Revelation, the total implosion of the social order as men utterly rebel against God and destroy themselves and the world in the process. Perhaps this is why Jesus said that unless those days were shortened, no one would survive (Matt. 24:22).

Religious Rebels

But we haven't gotten to the really bad news yet. That comes in 2 Timothy 3:5: "Having a form of godliness but denying its power. Have nothing to do with them." The word *form* means something like "having the outward appearance" of godliness. In the last days, as men turn away from God, paradoxically, they will become more religious, not less. Religion will become more popular as we approach the end times, because people will seek some refuge in a world that increasingly has lost its way. They will ask the right questions, but will follow the wrong answers. It will be religion for religion's sake, not religion for the sake of knowing Christ.

People will join the church (or some other religious organization), be baptized, attend the services, sing and pray and give and go through the motions, but their hearts will not be in it. They will deny the very power they profess to believe. In particular, they will embrace a kind of postmodern religion that allows them to do anything, believe anything, endorse anything, and live any way they choose as long as it makes them happy. They will say things like, "We don't need to be bound by the outdated rules of the Bible. Those were written two thousand years ago and don't apply to us today." That's not far-fetched. You can say things like that today and be elected a bishop in some denominations.

Notice how Paul says we are to respond to these false religious leaders: "Have nothing to do with them" (2 Tim. 3:5). That's clear, isn't it? It's also judgmental, narrow-minded, rude, unkind, unfair (in the eyes of many people), and a host of other things that are not politically correct today. But the Word of the Lord remains. We are to have nothing to do with religious people who do not believe the Bible and do not accept its authority over every area of life, including sexual morality. Such people are religious but lost.

During my years as a pastor in Oak Park, we were approached from time to time by nice people wondering why we wouldn't join in with all the other churches in Oak Park in various community endeavors. These wanted us to join hands with them and sing "Kum-Ba-Yah" and leave all the Jesus stuff alone so we wouldn't make anyone feel uncomfortable. Why would we not join them?

We did work side by side and hand in hand with true believers in Jesus who worship Him as Savior and Lord and who accept the Bible as the unquestioned Word of God. We fellowshipped and worked together in many ways with many groups, and we joined with a wide variety of evangelical ministries serving the greater Chicago area. But we would not join hands to work together with those who deny that Jesus is the only way to heaven, who are not born again, who do not accept the Bible, who do not preach salvation by grace alone through faith in Christ, who do not put the Bible above the shifting tide of public opinion. Evangelicals don't have much in common with theological liberals. They've got their religion and we've got ours. It is a good thing to work and worship together with those who share our common faith in the Lord Jesus Christ, but as for those who are religious but deny the fundamental truths of the faith, we should "have nothing to do with them."

SATAN IN THE LAST DAYS

Now war arose in heaven, Michael and his angels fighting against the dragon. And the dragon and his angels fought back, but he was defeated and there was no longer any place for them in heaven. And the great dragon was thrown down, that ancient serpent, who is called the devil and Satan, the deceiver of the whole world—he was thrown down to the earth, and his angels were thrown down with him. And I heard a loud voice in heaven, saying, "Now the salvation and the power and the kingdom of our God and the authority of his Christ have come, for the accuser of our brothers has been thrown down, who accuses them day and night before our God. And they have conquered him by the blood of the Lamb and by the word of their testimony, for they loved not their lives even unto death. Therefore, rejoice, O heavens and you who dwell in them! But woe to you, O earth and sea, for the devil has come down to you in great wrath, because he knows that his time is short!" (Rev. 12:7–12 ESV)

This passage describes a massive war in heaven in the last days. Throughout the galaxies the armies of God and of Satan fight one another. Fighting hand to hand, toe to toe, using weapons of warfare beyond anything known to man, the heavenly battle rages. Satan is strong, his armies well-trained, his tactics calculated to inflict the greatest harm possible. Yet slowly the tide of battle turns in favor of the forces of heaven. Inch by inch the good angels gain the high ground. Slowly, so slowly, Satan and his infernal henchmen find themselves being pushed to the edge of heaven. Finally, with a great shout the angels of God see their opening and pour through the breach, routing the demons from the fields of heaven.

Revelation 12:8 contains a wonderful phrase we must not miss: "He was defeated" (ESV). Satan was not strong enough. In the end, he has to give ground. That Infernal Liar, that Great Pretender, that Bloodthirsty Opponent of All That Is Good, that Big-Mouthed Boaster, that Roaring Lion is revealed in the end to be "not strong enough" (v. 8). Let us learn a great lesson. Satan is never strong enough. Every time he fights against God, he loses. When we fight him alone, we always lose. But when he fights God, he always loses. So when we fight Satan in the power of almighty God, we will win and he will lose. Although he is strong, he is not strong enough!

He lost the battle. When he lost, his demons lost with him. He was hurled down to the earth, and his angels were hurled down with him. Here is a picture of utter and total defeat. He was tossed out of heaven like yesterday's garbage. If this is a battle for Dodge City, Marshall Dillon has just tossed the bad guys through the saloon window and out into the street.

Satan is angry. His time is short. He has been cast to the earth. He is like a wounded, cornered, snarling beast. Soon he will be destroyed. But before he goes, he's going to hurt as many people as possible. He's like a maniacal killer who has been cornered on the third floor of an apartment house. He's surrounded by more than one hundred police officers. He's been wounded twice and is bleeding profusely. But he's holding seven people hostage. He knows he'll never make it out alive. No point in making a deal. Filled with rage, he begins to shoot his victims one by one.

Revelation 12 is the "story behind the story." It explains why in the last days "terrible times" will come on the earth. Satan will unleash his full fury in every direction. Thus we will see outbreaks of evil on a scale unprecedented in human history.

But we must consider one more important piece in order to understand what spiritual warfare will look like in the last days.

THE SPIRITUAL HARVEST OF THE LAST DAYS

Jesus told a story about a farmer who sowed wheat in his field, but during the night his enemy came and sowed weeds (sometimes called tares) among the wheat. The farmer had no idea what had happened until weeks later when he discovered the wheat and the weeds growing together. When his servants volunteered to pull up the weeds, he told them to leave the weeds alone lest they accidentally pull up the wheat at the same time. They were to let the wheat and weeds grow together until the harvest, at which time he would have the reapers gather the weeds for burning, and the wheat would be gathered into the barn (Matt. 13:24–30, 36–43).

Later Jesus' disciples asked Him to explain the story. The wheat and the weeds represent believers and unbelievers in the world. The Lord sows the good seed that produces believers, while the devil sows bad seed that produces unbelievers. That's the world as we see it today. Christians and non-Christians live and work and play side by side. We shop at the same stores, we eat at the same restaurants, we drive on the same roads, and we work in the same companies. Very often we watch the same programs on TV, and we may even send our children to the same schools.

The real point of the story is that you can't always tell by looking at the outside who is a Christian and who is an unbeliever. Superficially we may appear to be much the same. And when we die, most of us are buried in the ground. I've walked through many cemeteries, and you can't tell much about the spiritual state of those who rest six feet below the surface. The saved and the lost lie side by side. We are much the same in life and in death. But a day of final separation is coming when the Lord Himself will send His angels to separate the righteous from the unrighteous. Since He alone will be the judge, there will be no mistakes.

Now let us ask what this parable teaches us about the last days. I think it suggests that there will be parallel harvests of good and evil in the days preceding the coming of the Lord. Evil will be more outrageous than ever before, and the good will be easier to spot. Evildoers will become more brazen, and there will be a corresponding harvest of righteousness. The Lord's work will prosper in the midst of continuing moral decline. This leads me to believe that the greatest revivals in history are still ahead of us. We've all heard it said that the darker the night, the brighter the light shines. When a jeweler wants to convince you of the brilliance of a diamond, he places it against a black background.

It is sometimes said that those of us who believe in the premillennial return of Christ are too pessimistic about the future. I personally don't feel pessimistic at all. If we are indeed living in the last days before the return of Christ, we should expect things to get better and worse at the same time. I think we should believe God for amazing answers to prayer, culture-shaking moves of the Holy Spirit, and unprecedented open doors for evangelism. We should pray for the gospel to spread like wildfire across India and China.

If there is going to be a final harvest of righteousness, then we should expect to see hundreds of millions of people coming to Christ in the years to come. And at the same time, the devil will do all he can to ignite an explosion of evil around the world.

The Church in China

I had a long conversation with a young man who teaches English in China. Speaking very carefully (because conversations can be monitored), he said that there has been a recent awakening in a certain province that led to some very high-profile people coming to Christ. In response, a Community Party official sent a very specific warning to the English teachers that they were in China to teach English, not to do evangelism.

When people ask about the state of the Christian movement in China, there is no quick or easy answer. Officially China remains atheistic even though the government tolerates a certain amount of religious activity. In recent years, as China has aggressively entered the global marketplace, in some places there is a measure of freedom. In other places, official opposition and harassment of Christians has actually increased. One wise leader told me, "Remember, China is a huge country. Everything you hear about it is true somewhere." The issue of religious freedom depends very much on who you are and where you are and who you know and how open people are.

In response to the burgeoning house church movement, the authorities have begun a crackdown even though they cannot hope to stop (or even greatly slow down) the spread of small groups meeting in houses and apartments all over China. In talking about all this, the young man pointed me to Habakkuk 2. Read that, he said. Read it and think about it carefully. Read verse 12 with its warning to pagan empires built on bloodshed: "Woe to him who builds a town with blood and founds a city on iniquity!" (ESV).

The prophet aims his words at the ancient Babylonian Empire, which in its day conquered the ancient Near East through hitherto unknown violence and rapacious cruelty. It is said that the

Babylonians piled up the skulls of their enemies as a warning to those who dared to oppose them. But those words apply to every evil empire of history. Those who profit by murder will one day be brought low. Such a thought must have seemed impossible to Habakkuk's first readers. Every human empire seems invincible at its zenith. But the roll call of fallen empires stands for all to see: Babylon. Medo-Persia. Greece. Rome.

In 1817 Percy Bysshe Shelley penned the classic poem *Ozymandias* to demonstrate the arrogance of those who believe their earthly empires will last forever:

> *I met a traveler from an antique land*
> *Who said: Two vast and trunkless legs of stone*
> *Stand in the desert. Near them, on the sand,*
> *Half sunk, a shattered visage lies, whose frown,*
> *And wrinkled lip, and sneer of cold command,*
> *Tell that its sculptor well those passions read,*
> *Which yet survive, stamped on these lifeless things,*
> *The hand that mocked them, and the heart that fed,*
> *And on the pedestal these words appear:*
> *"My name is Ozymandias, King of Kings:*
> *Look upon my works, ye Mighty, and despair!"*
> *Nothing beside remains. Round the decay*
> *Of that colossal wreck, boundless and bare*
> *The lone and level sands stretch far away.*

Ponder the irony of a statue in the desert, surrounded by nothing but the drifting sands. When Ozymandias calls on the mighty to despair, he means that they should live in fear of his power, yet nothing remains of his vast empire but the scattered ruins of the stones that form a "colossal wreck" in the wilderness. Those who think they are invincible should themselves despair. The mightiest empires will one day be brought to the ground.

The young man in China earnestly reminded me, "When the Communists came to power in China in 1949, they expelled all the foreign missionaries. Back then there were seven hundred thousand Christians. For decades no one knew what was happening to the church or if it even survived. But by 1980 there were at least ten million Christians in China. Today there may be as many as one hundred million." Then he quoted Habakkuk 2:14 with its vision of the knowledge of the Lord spreading across the earth "as the waters cover the sea." "It's already happening," he said. "Nothing can stop it. There is no power, no policy, and there are no pundits that can reverse what God is doing." The ultimate fulfillment of this verse awaits the return of Christ to the earth to establish His kingdom. But as we race headlong toward the final days of this age, we should not be surprised—indeed, we should expect—that there will be an explosion of gospel preaching around the world with untold multitudes coming to Christ.

In the Whole Earth

Matthew 24:14 says, "This gospel of the kingdom will be preached in the whole world as a testimony to all nations, and then the end will come." Sometimes this verse is exclusively applied to the preaching of the gospel during the tribulation period. While that may be its major thrust, it certainly applies as well to the period preceding the tribulation.

One mark of the last days is that the gospel will go forth to all the nations of the earth. Remember that "nations" in Matthew 24:14 does not refer primarily to political entities, but to the various "people groups" of the world. The gospel is preached to *all* the nations of the world. *Then* (and only then) does the end come. According to Jesus, the end cannot come until all the nations have heard the gospel message.

Does this mean that every single person must hear the gospel message? No. Does it mean that the world must become Christian? No. It means that the gospel must be preached in every nation.

What, in a practical sense, does that entail? It means that as we approach the end times, there will be a marked increase in the tempo of world evangelization, a renewed interest in fulfilling the

Great Commission, a new sense of urgency for the missionary enterprise, and a new focus on reaching the unreached people groups of the world. And that is exactly what we see as we enter the twenty-first century. According to the Joshua Project Web site, out of a world population of 6.5 billion, 2.58 billion (or 39.6 percent) are considered unreached or least reached. Out of 15,956 people groups in the world, 6,625 fall into the category of unreached or least reached. The good news is that 95 percent of the world's population has access to the gospel through Bible translations, the Jesus film, and other Christian media.[3]

The gospel is going forth today in more ways to more people by more people in more nations than ever before. All of this fits precisely what Jesus predicted for the last days. As we near the end of this age, we will see a rapidly increasing tempo of world evangelization as the gospel goes out to every nation and the final harvest of souls begins.

It will be the best of times.

It will be the worst of times.

Abandoning the Faith

Note carefully what 1 Timothy 4:1 says: "The Spirit clearly says that in later times some will abandon the faith and follow deceiving spirits and things taught by demons." Ours is not the first generation to be faced with counterfeit Christianity.

A glance at church history reveals that the early church faced a long series of spiritual counterfeits. Pick up a history book and you find names like the Docetics, the Gnostics, the Cerinthians, the Arians, the Nicolaitans, the Marcionites, the Nestorians, the Ebionites, and the Sabellians. Those are just dusty names to us, but to the early Christians they were real flesh-and-blood heretics who tried to peddle a distorted version of Christianity. That's why there were so many church councils in the first few centuries.

The church had to hammer out its faith on the anvil of doctrinal controversy. That's why you find so many warnings in the New Testament concerning false teachers in the church. Virtually every

New Testament book contains one. Some of the major references are: Matthew 24:4–5, 24; Acts 20:29–30; Romans 16:17–19; 2 Corinthians 11:13–15; Galatians 1:6–9; Philippians 3:1–2; Colossians 2:4, 8, 18, 20–23; 2 Thessalonians 2:1–3; 1 Timothy 1:3–7; 4:1–6; 2 Timothy 3:1–9; 4:3–4; 2 Peter 2:1–3; 1 John 2:18–19; 2 John 7–11; Jude 3–4; Revelation 2:6, 14–15, 20–24. Clearly, the early church took very seriously the threat posed by those who would add to or subtract from the original faith handed down from the apostles.

Jesus warned us that "many will come in my name, claiming, 'I am the Christ,' and will deceive many" (Matt. 24:5). And Paul, writing in 2 Thessalonians 2:9–10, says that the Antichrist will display the work of Satan by using "all kinds of counterfeit miracles, signs and wonders." He will be so successful at mimicking the work of God through his "miracles" that millions of people will follow him to their ultimate destruction.

Taken together, these verses paint a picture of unprecedented religious apostasy in the last days. They especially apply to so-called Christian leaders who depart from the Christian faith. These are the leaders who deny the inerrancy of the Bible, deny the necessity for the blood atonement, deny the virgin birth, deny the lostness of all people, deny the reality of eternal hell, deny that those who die without Jesus Christ are lost forever. They turn away after fads and popular social causes and pander to the powers that be. They support the killing of unborn babies, support gay rights, support the right of pornographers to practice their evil trade. They do not preach the gospel because they do not even believe the gospel. They are wolves in sheep's clothing. The pulpits of America are increasingly filled with such religious charlatans.

Many of the mainline churches are in serious trouble because they have followed the line of least resistance in terms of doctrine and morality. One has only to think of the ongoing debate over homosexuality in the Episcopal Church, which in 2006 elected Katharine Jefferts Schori, who had voted to elect openly homosexual Gene Robinson as bishop of New Hampshire, as presiding bishop. In a chapter at the General Convention in Columbus, Ohio, she referred to "Mother Jesus," thus effectively transgendering the Son of God. R. Andrew Newman tells how it happened:

> *At the convention's closing Eucharist, the new presiding bishop preached, "Colossians calls Jesus the firstborn of all creation, the firstborn from the dead. That sweaty, bloody, tear-stained labor of the cross bears new life. Our mother Jesus gives birth to a new creation—and you and I are His children."*

Our mother Jesus?

> *Bishop Schori felt no need to cloak her language so as not to scandalize the average Episcopalian. Tossing aside the New Testament, she transgendered the Lord without a qualm in the world—and for all the world to hear.*[4]

In an interview with CNN, when Schori was asked if it is a sin to be homosexual, she replied,

> *"I don't believe so. I believe that God creates us with different gifts. Each one of us comes into this world with a different collection of things that challenge us and things that give us joy and allow us to bless the world around us. Some people come into this world with affections ordered toward other people of the same gender and some people come into this world with affections directed at people of the other gender."*[5]

Cal Thomas addresses the matter this way:

> *Maybe the question for Bishop Schori and her fellow heretics should be: if homosexual practice is not sin, what is? And how do we know? Or is it a matter of "thus saith the opinion polls" and lobbying groups, rather than "thus saith the Lord"? With*

the bishop's "doctrine" of inclusion, why exclude anyone? How
about applying the religious equivalent of "open borders" and
let everyone into the church, including unrepentant prostitutes,
murderers, liars, thieves and atheists. If the Episcopal Church
denies what is clearly taught in scripture about important mat-
ters like sexual behavior, why expect its leaders to have any con-
victions about anything, including directions to Heaven? How
can anyone be sure, if the guidebook is so full of errors?[6]

His conclusion is short and to the point: "Conservative Episcopalians are too few in number to stop the theological drift. If they intend to preserve their congregations without further theological seepage, they should 'come out from among them and be separate.'"[7]

The Presbyterians (PCUSA) have the same problem, plus now we are being told that the Holy Trinity is sexist because of the masculine terms Father and Son. My brother sent me an editorial cartoon that shows four contestants playing a game called "Name That Trinity" under a banner reading, "Presbyterian Church USA General Assembly." The first person says, "Father, Son and Holy Spirit," the second says, "Mother, Child and Womb," the third says, "Rock, Redeemer, Friend," and the fourth says, "Rock, Paper, Scissors." The caption reads, "Bad news. We just got word the Episcopalians are praying for us!"

Once you leave the solid rock of biblical authority, you step into the quicksand of shifting public opinion where anything goes and no one can tell you that you are wrong. The doctrinal defection runs deep, and across the country true believers inside those denominations have tough choices to make. But that should not surprise us. The Bible predicts a great wave of religious apostasy in the last days. As Dr. Walvoord says, all this simply prepares the world to follow the Antichrist when he is finally revealed.

What will spiritual warfare look like in the last days? Expect the devil to pull out all the stops because he knows his time is short. Asymmetric warfare will increase in intensity as we approach the coming of Christ. Look for the stakes to be raised and the battle to be joined on every front. War on earth. War in heaven.

Tough times are coming. Don't be surprised.

There will be great days for evangelism. Be ready.

You may face opposition. Be bold. Jesus is coming! Travel light.

Let me go back to the words of Eugene Peterson. God is shaking the kingdoms of the earth so that what is unshakable will remain. "Getting rid of all the historical and religious junk so that the unshakable essentials stand clear and uncluttered" (Heb. 12:27 THE MESSAGE).

It's time to do some spiritual housecleaning. Time to look under the rug and behind the couch. Time to vacuum the corners of your soul. Time to clean out the rec room. Time to seal the cracks in the foundation. Time to shore up the sagging walls of your heart.

Romans 11:20 puts it very succinctly: "You stand by faith." Paul means more by this than simply believing the right things. Standing by faith means that you have received God's mercy, confessed your sin, and run to the cross for forgiveness. But even that is not the end of it. To stand by faith means that you live each day by faith, trusting in God's mercy to you in Jesus Christ, knowing that you have no other hope.

When I preached at a conference in Colorado Springs, I remarked that Lewis Sperry Chafer defined faith as trusting in Christ so much that if He can't take me to heaven, I'm not going there. Erwin Lutzer, pastor of Moody Church in Chicago, who was also speaking at the conference, told me afterward that Chafer had said it in a more shocking way. He said that when he dies, if God asks him, "Why should I let you into heaven?" he will reply, "I am trusting in Jesus Christ and Him alone for my salvation." At that point if God says, "That's not enough," Chafer said, "I will simply walk away and burn in hell forever." He was right to say that. If faith in Christ is not enough to get me into heaven, then I too will go to hell because I have no Plan B. Jesus is my only hope. I am living and dying by faith in Him.

My hope is built on nothing less
Than Jesus' blood and righteousness.
I dare not trust the sweetest frame,
But wholly lean on Jesus' name.

On Christ the solid rock I stand.
All other ground is sinking sand,
All other ground is sinking sand.

Can you say that? When you stand at the gate of heaven and God says, "Why should I let you in?" what answer will you give?

"I was a member of Wesley Methodist Church." Not good enough.

"I was an elder at Wayside Chapel." You'll be in big trouble.

"My father built our church." That's good, but it's not the right answer.

"I lived a good life." We're happy for you, but you weren't good enough.

"I gave to feed the orphans in Namibia." That's truly wonderful, but that won't open the doors of heaven.

"I was baptized by Father O'Reilly." I'm sure he was a good man, but that's not enough.

"I read *The Purpose-Driven Life* five times." That won't get you to heaven.

"I listen to Christian radio every day." That's admirable, but it's not the right answer.

If you want to go to heaven, you must trust in Jesus Christ and Him alone. You must go "all in" on the Son of God who loved you and died for you. You must believe in Him so much that if He can't take you to heaven, you aren't going to go there.

We are saved by grace, we stand by faith, and we depend completely on the mercy of our Lord Jesus Christ. Don't be proud or cocky or arrogant. If you make it to heaven, it will only be because of God's kindness toward you. And between now and then, stand by faith. Live by faith. Walk by faith. Run to the cross every day. Lay hold of Christ and never let go.

WHAT DIFFERENCE DOES IT MAKE?

I have a friend who is not given to speculative comments. My friend is not the sort to say, "The world is ending soon." Yet several times this person has said to me, "I believe the world is ending soon." Is it? Perhaps it is. We will know the answer soon enough. If the world ends tomorrow, then my friend was right! And I do think this might indeed be the beginning of the end, so to speak. Suppose that Jesus is coming soon. How then should we live?

Be Alert!

The last days will be a time of confusion and spiritual delusion. Don't be sucked in by the spirit of the antichrist that is already in the world. That spirit tries to make us think that sin isn't really sinful and that there is no such thing as right and wrong. It also seduces us into silence when we ought to be speaking out. Ponder the words of 1 Peter 5:8, "Be sober-minded; be watchful. Your adversary the devil prowls around like a roaring lion, seeking someone to devour" (ESV). Don't let that "someone" be you. A great deception will come to the earth in the last days. Many will be deceived. It's easy to say, "That would never happen to me." Don't be too sure. Many will be deceived who today would laugh at that suggestion.

This is no time to play church. It's time to get serious with the Lord. This is no time just to be religious. It's time to get right with God. This is no time to go through the motions. It's time to make Jesus first in your life.

Don't Be Naive

This is a time for the people of God to be "wise as serpents and harmless as doves" (see Matt. 10:16). Don't be naive about the true nature of sin. Bad things happen because evil people cause them to happen. They hijack planes and fly them into skyscrapers. They mail anthrax to public officials. They strap bombs on young people, who then blow themselves up on a crowded bus. They loot and kill and destroy and defraud and break the laws of God and man, and sometimes they go on TV and gloat about it. If we are indeed living near the coming of Christ, then we ought to brace ourselves for further outbreaks of hideous evil. The worst is yet to come. No matter how good the world seems to be in terms of technology, the moral compass is pointing in the wrong direction.

Be Bold

This is no time for compromise. In times like these, Christians ought to be bold and open about our faith. Raise the flag of Jesus high above your head, and then take your stand under that flag so that those near and far know who you are and whose you are. Open your mouth and say a good word for the Lord. Speak up for the Savior. Let your voice be heard so loudly that no one can doubt whose side you are on.

March in Tight Formation

This is no time for believers to wander off on their own. Stay tight with your brothers and sisters in Christ. Stay tight with your local church. Stay tight with your Sunday school class or your small group. Stay tight with your Christian friends at work. Stay tight so you can't be easily picked off by the Enemy. When we march in tight formation, we are a formidable force to be reckoned with. When we try to go it alone, we become easy targets for Satan's attacks.

Live Without Fear

If we know the Lord, we are joined with the One who is the ultimate victor in the battle between good and evil. One of the Negro spirituals says, "My Lord, what a morning, when the stars fall from the skies." The slaves often sang songs that talked about the coming of the Lord because that great hope contrasted so vividly with the bleakness of their bondage. If we read about "perilous times" to come and then give in to fear, we have missed the great point that Jesus is the victor in the end. We must live in hope because our God is a God of hope, and in Christ we have great hope for the future. The church has always done its best work in bad days and hard times. When the skies are the darkest, it is then that the glory of the gospel shines the brightest.

These are great days to be alive, the greatest days in all human history. Think of it. We may live to see Jesus returning in power and great glory.

We are fighting a battle we cannot lose. The Lord is looking for some soldiers who will serve in His army. Will you answer the call?

CONCLUSION

"We are given one life, and the decision is ours whether to wait for circumstances to make up our mind, or whether to act, and in acting, to live."

——GENERAL OMAR BRADLEY[1]

SEVERAL MONTHS AGO a group of college students came to visit us. Around the breakfast table we started talking about asymmetric spiritual warfare. That led to a long discussion about how Satan attacks us in multiple ways, he rarely hits us head-on, and he attacks from many directions at once, with the ultimate goal of discouraging us. Various team members told how they had been struggling with discouragement. From there we talked about the importance of sticking close to our brothers and sisters who are in the battle with us, how that if a soldier gets separated from his squad, he's in big trouble.

A young man spoke up and told us something he learned while serving with the Marines in Iraq. During his tour of duty, he was stationed in Fallujah, the scene of some of the worst fighting. His sergeant used to tell them, "Two is one, one is none, and if you are by yourself, you're done." When the time comes to go to battle, you can't wander off on your own, or you'll soon be in big trouble. But "two is one" if you stick together. And "one is none" if you don't. That's excellent advice for the spiritual battles we all face. Remember, if Satan can discourage you, he's already won the battle. Don't fight him alone. Stay tight with your brothers and sisters because two is one, and one is none when you fight against the Enemy of your soul.

This is always important, but never more so than when we face asymmetric spiritual warfare. We are stronger together than we are alone. We can stand strong when we stand together. The Greeks understood this principle when they developed the phalanx in 700 B.C. By massing armed soldiers closely together, they multiplied their effectiveness as a fighting force. Standing shoulder to shoulder with shields raised provided protection from enemy attack. Yet if one of those soldiers was separated from the phalanx, he became an easy target.

Solomon reminds us of this truth in Ecclesiastes 4:9–12 (THE MESSAGE):

> It's better to have a partner than go it alone. Share the work, share the wealth. And if one falls down, the other helps, but if there's no one to help, tough! Two in a bed warm each other. Alone, you shiver all night. By yourself you're unprotected. With a friend you can face the worst. Can you round up a third?

We need each other more than we know. When we are suddenly attacked, if we are alone, it is easy to be discouraged and feel like giving up. But if we know that others are cheering for us and are there to help us, we can find the strength to keep on going even in the worst of times.

As I was nearing the end of this manuscript, I ate supper with a friend who leads a weekly men's Bible study. Part of their accountability involves five specific commitments. If a man has successfully completed them, he will be able to say "Seven, seven, seven, yes, yes." That means he has spent . . .

Seven minutes a day in prayer.
Seven minutes reading his Bible.
Seven minutes reading the book the group is studying.
Yes, he contacted his accountability partner in the group.
Yes, he attempted to start a kingdom conversation.[2]

The men are paired off and agree to contact each other weekly to ask these questions:

1. Have you been with a woman anywhere this past week that might be seen as compromising?

2. Have any of your financial dealings lacked integrity?

3. Have you intentionally exposed yourself to any sexually explicit material?

4. Have you been faithful to your wife in your words, thoughts, and actions?

5. Have you spent adequate time in Bible study and prayer?

6. Have you given priority time to your family?

7. Have you handled hurt and frustration well this week?

8. Have you just lied to me?

Then there are two final questions:

9. Have you started a kingdom conversation this week? Tell me about it.

10. Have you prayed daily for the people God has laid it on your heart to witness to in the near future?

Every day we have important choices to make, but there is one choice we *don't* have. The invisible war rages all around us whether we see it or not. All of us are soldiers on the front lines of spiritual combat. Not only is our Enemy cunning, he is also much smarter than we are. He waits for a weak moment when we are unprepared, and then he pounces on us. Then we wonder why we are defeated yet again.

It doesn't have to be that way. God has provided all the resources necessary for you to win the battle for your soul. It won't be easy or automatic, and you can't do it alone. But if you take up the weapons God supplies, and if you lean hard on your Christian friends; and if you give thanks when you feel like giving up, you will find that real victory is possible in the thousand daily skirmishes and the occasional big battles you face.

Let this be our final thought. Satan is the ultimate loser. You may have heard the saying, "I've read the end of the Book and we win!" That says it all. If you've read Revelation, you know Jesus wins in the end, and He wins big! And everyone joined by faith with Jesus wins, because He is the captain of our salvation. When the captain wins, the whole team wins. The forces of evil cannot stand against Him. He speaks the word and they are banished forever. Read it for yourself. Jesus wins! The devil loses! And all those on the devil's side lose with him. That includes the demons, every worker of iniquity, all the various ranks of evil spirits, and all those who have wittingly or unwittingly done the devil's bidding on the earth.

There is great hope at the end of the day for all those who struggle against sin. On Easter Sunday morning the word came down from heaven to the devil and all his demons: Turn out the lights; the party's over.

Do you feel defeated or discouraged? Stand and fight. Have you been tempted to give in? Stand and fight. Are you wavering between right and wrong? Stand and fight.

Remember this. The captain of our salvation has already won the battle. Satan can harass you, but he cannot destroy you.

Lo! His doom is sure; one little word shall fell him.

NOTES

Chapter 1: A New Name for a Very Old War

1. "'Asymmetric Warfare': The USS Cole, and the Intifada," *The Estimate*, vol. XII, no. 22, 3 November 2000, http://www.theestimate.com/public/110300. html.

2. Michael Novak, "Global Liberty," http://www.nationalreview.com/novak/ novak200501200814.asp.

3. Richard Thieme, "Battlespace," http://www.thiemeworks.com/islands/ archive/20011004.html.

4. Erwin Lutzer, *The Serpent of Paradise* (Chicago: Moody, 1996), 102.

5. Ibid., 98.

6. Michael Green, *I Believe in Satan's Downfall* (Grand Rapids, Mich.: Eerdmans), 253.

Chapter 3: War in Heavenly Places

1. Geoff Thomas, "Cyrus: The Return and the Future," http://www. alfredplacechurch.org.uk/sermons/dan10.htm.

2. Robert Odom, "The Depth of the Call," *LoveINC Newsletter*, Fall 2006, 2.

3. Geoff Thomas, "Cyrus: The Return and the Future."

4. You can find the entire report of our trip to Haiti online at http://www. keepbelieving.com/sermons/read_sermon.asp?id=647.

Chapter 4: The Devil's Foothold

1. Harold Hoehner, *Ephesians: An Exegetical Commentary* (Grand Rapids, Mich.: Baker, 2002), 639–40.

2. Richard Wurmbrand, *Voice of the Martyrs*, December 1998.

Chapter 5: Lessons from Chairman Mao

1. Mao Tse-tung, *Quotations from Chairman Mao Tse-tung*, no publication data given. Purchased in Beijing, China, January 2006. All quotes are from this edition.

2. Jung Chang and Jon Halliday, *Mao: The Unknown Story* (New York: Knopf, 2005), 3.

Chapter 7: Forward-Leaning Defense

1. Michael Novak, "Global Liberty," http://www.nationalreview.com/novak/ novak200501200814.asp.

2. Ibid.

3. Portions of this chapter first appeared as an article in *Moody Magazine*, "From Temptation to Triumph," March/April 1998.

Chapter 8: Singing Your Way to Victory

1. www.battlefocused.org.

2. John Piper, "Ambushing Satan with Song," http://www.desiringgod.org/ ResourceLibrary/Sermons/ByScripture/47/474_Ambushing_Satan_with_Song/.

Chapter 9: Cataclysmic Times

1. Wayne Biddle, "Anger: Rage Beneficial," *Johns Hopkins Magazine*, September 2005, http://www.jhu.edu/~jhumag/0905web/anger1.html (accessed 28 July 2006).

2. Ibid.

3. http://www.joshuaproject.net.

4. R. Andrew Newman, "Our Mother Jesus," www.nationalreview.com, 27 June 2006.

5. Interview found online at http://transcripts.cnn.com/TRANSCRIPTS/0606/ 19/lol.04.html.

6. Cal Thomas, "Church Lite," 22 June 2006, http://jewishworldreview.com/cols/thomas062206.asp.

7. Ibid.

Conclusion

1. http://www.answers.com/topic/omar-bradley.

2. Duke Heller, *How to Start a Kingdom Conversation* (Winona Lake, Ind.: BMH Books, 2005).

SPECIAL NOTE

If you would like to contact the author,
you can reach him in the following ways:

By letter:
Ray Pritchard
P.O. Box 257
Elmhurst, IL 60126

By e-mail: Ray@keepbelieving.com
Via the Internet: www.keepbelieving.com

An Anchor for the Soul Series

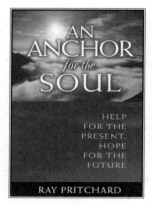

ISBN: 0-8024-1535-0

Anchor for the Soul

An Anchor for the Soul is a straight-forward, easily readable book—the perfect introduction for those just beginning their Christian journey, or for those considering new steps toward God.

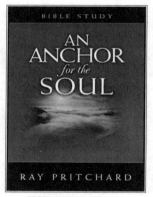

ISBN: 0-8024-1510-5

Anchor for the Soul Bible Study

Have you ever wondered . . .
What is God like?
How can we really know Him?
Ray Pritchard reveals the answers to these honest and important questions through the good news of the gospel. It is possible to know God deeply and personally. All you have to do is have the desire to know Him, and, by knowing God, you can experience His power in your life.

MOODY
PUBLISHERS

THE NAME YOU CAN TRUST.

1-800-678-6928 www.MoodyPublishers.org